INDOCHINESTYLE

INDOCHINESTYLE

TEXT BY **BARBARA WALKER** PHOTOGRAPHS BY **JAY GRAHAM**

Marshall Cavendish
Editions

Copyright © 2019, 2011 Marshall Cavendish International (Asia) Private Limited

First published in 2011

This paperback edition published in 2019 by Marshall Cavendish Editions
An imprint of Marshall Cavendish International

A member of the
Times Publishing Group

Other Marshall Cavendish Offices
Marshall Cavendish Corporation, 99 White Plains Road, Tarrytown NY 10591-9001, USA • Marshall
Cavendish International (Thailand) Co Ltd, 253 Asoke, 12th Flr, Sukhumvit 21 Road, Klongtoey Nua,
Wattana, Bangkok 10110, Thailand • Marshall Cavendish (Malaysia) Sdn Bhd, Times Subang, Lot 46,
Subang Hi-Tech Industrial Park, Batu Tiga, 40000 Shah Alam, Selangor Darul Ehsan, Malaysia.

Marshall Cavendish is a registered trademark of Times Publishing Limited

National Library Board (Singapore) Cataloguing-in-Publication Data
Name(s): Walker, Barbara. | Graham, Jay, 1946-, photographer.
Title: Indochine Style / text by Barbara Walker; photographs by Jay Graham.
Description: Singapore: Marshall Cavendish Editions, 2019. | First published: 2011.
Identifier(s): OCN 1090357303 | ISBN 978-981-4841-98-6 (paperback)
Subject(s): LCSH: Architecture—Vietnam. | Architecture—Laos. | Interior architecture—Vietnam. |
Interior architecture—Laos.
Classification: DDC 720.9597—dc23

Printed in Singapore

FRONT COVER Lotus-shaped lampshade at the Vine Wine Boutique Bar and Café in HaNoi.
PAGE 1 Natural rattan furniture, silk lanterns and patterned floors at Maxim's nam an, SaiGon.
PAGE 2 Stylish 1920s grille-work at Le Madraux café and furniture shop in the Old Quarter of HaNoi.
THIS PAGE Period Art Deco furnishings in the home of LIM Du Minh near SaiGon.
FOLLOWING PAGE Indochine-style salon and dining room in the home of the family of Mai Lam.
PAGE 8-9 Women in the Red River delta planting rice wearing the traditional hat, the *non*.
PAGE 10 Vintage furnishings and needlework pillow covers at Nguyen Freres, HaNoi.

For the people of Indochina, who have valiantly protected their cultural heritage; and Thanh and Nathan, my surrogate family in VietNam

Contents

Introduction

Indochine Style…a style that conjures images of tropical nights astir
with amber lights glowing through portals with slanted louvres;
of rich jewel-toned colors softened by tangles of lush equatorial
plants that perfume the sultry air. With romantic ideals at its heart,
Indochine Style is about the nostalgia for a bygone era of grandeur.

edginess that takes the movement from the sultry place of its origin to global acceptance. There is a spontaneous mix of disparate objects that brings an otherwise eclectic jumble to an integrated whole. Often the style interacts as a foil, the element that mingles with other designs to give an unexplainable panache more easily felt than described.

A glimpse inside the louvered openings of an Indochine salon reveals sumptuous furnishings; perhaps Louis XV *fauteuil* chairs grouped with casual rattan furniture, all daringly upholstered in silks and velvets lavishly adorned with the richest of passementerie. Jasmine and tamarind perfume the humid air enhancing the audacious intensity of the lavish colors of Indochine, softened only by the lush greens of the tropics. Here is a style that ignores past rules by presuming that elegance and grandeur may coexist with inherent simplicity and comfort—in fact not only coexist but unite to create a harmonious and cultivated purity made manifest in architecture, textiles, furniture, arts, and crafts.

Indochina endures in imaginations as a place of mystery and intrigue; a place that arouses romantic images of the unknown made legendary by film and literature. While entangled with notions of the rare and exotic, the Style's organic designs are not caught in the lush jungles of its birthplace; they are a leitmotif central to Southeast Asian arts and architecture.

Antique maps and historical records considered Indochina a peninsula extending from the southern borders of China; bounded

INDOCHINE STYLE is a movement set into motion during that relatively short period of time—the late 1800's to 1954—when the Empire of France colonized Laos, Cambodia, and VietNam forming French Indochina. Design concepts that flowed from these consolidated lands embraced perspectives of the Orient with a difference, there was a subtle influence of French refinement. The elements and motifs from Indochina infused an exotic presence in the decorative arts, home furnishings, architecture, fashion, and the visual arts. Today, after a century of global acceptance, Indochine Style is often recognized as East-West fusion.

Indochine Style is definable in what may seem incompatible ingredients— natural simplicity deli-berately mixed with sophistication— nevertheless it is this very

PREVIOUS PAGES *(left)* **A garden path lined with native bamboo, winds past Vietnamese-made jardiniere toward a mango-colored house on the property of LIM Du Minh, near SaiGon;** *(right)* **Map of Indochina.**

by the South China Sea on the east and included the countries of Siam, the Malay Peninsula, Laos, Cambodia, Burma, North and South VietNam. French Indochina was formed in 1887 under the name L'Indochine française colonizing Laos, Cambodia, and VietNam. France's interests in Cambodia were limited; therefore the focus of this book, *Indochine Style*, centers on VietNam and Laos.

"...Indochina mainly meant VietNam, and that Cambodia and Laos tended to be eclipsed behind France's administrative focus on VietNam. And this led equally to a cultural focus which tended either to ignore the particularities of Cambodia and Laos, or to subsume their specific identities under the umbrella term Indochine française."
— *France In Indochina: Colonial Encounters* by Nicola Cooper

The emergence of Indochine style at the turn of the 20th century is linked to an international change in design and lifestyle preferences, a transition in the West from European Classicism to enthusiasm for things of an Oriental nature. A path for Indochine Style may be traced to the late Middle Ages by the most popular book in medieval Europe, commonly called *Il Millione*, (The Million Lies), also known as *The Travels of Marco Polo*. Polo had returned to Italy in 1295 after a voyage of more than 20 years that took him throughout the Far East. Imprisoned by the Genoese following a sea-battle with the Venetians, Polo made good use of his incarceration by dictating stories of his adventures to cellmate Rustacian de Pise, an Italian writer of romantic stories. His stories told of Emperor Kublai Khan welcoming young Marco Polo to the royal courts,

OPPOSITE Rising from the cool green waters of Halong Bay in the Gulf of Tonkin are the limestone formations (*karst*). Halong Bay is designated a World Heritage site by UNESCO. Here a serene view of Halong Bay is enjoyed from the steamer chairs on the *Emeraude*, a reproduction of a paddlewheel boat named the same during the French Colonial period.

BELOW The ship *Emeraude* plied the South China Sea transporting passengers along the long coast of VietNam and into the Mekong River delta. This image shows the newly built *Emeraude* moored among one of the numerous boat villages in Halong Bay.

The vast network of rivers in Indochina have always provided a primary means of getting around. These young boys row their hand-woven basket boat on the Perfume River just as their ancestors have done since ancient times.

engaging him as a special envoy throughout China, India, and Burma. Polo returned to Venice describing the glorious riches he had seen, the exotic people living in China where they used paper money for trade, bathed up to three times per week in heated bathrooms, and made a delicious wine from rice. As a last word in defense of his stories while adding fuel to the fires his tales had lighted, Marco Polo uttered from his deathbed: "I have not told one-half of what I really saw". While the stories were considered phantasmal in the Middle Ages, they ignited a fascination with this unimaginable place that demanded further discovery, and the great period of maritime trade began.

By the 15th century, The Golden Age of Sea exploration and trading extended to the Indonesian Archipelago and on into the forbidden Far East. After months and years

at sea, great-masted schooners sailed back to their homelands laden with precious cargoes of ivories, paper-thin porcelains, mirror-finished lacquers, embroideries, and glorious silks in the most luxurious colors. Geographically, Indo-china caught the attention of world traders because of its fortunate position at an intersection in the shipping lanes and its network of mighty rivers. Bernard Groslier captured this essence in his book *Indochina—Archaeologia Mundi:* "Indochina is like a fan, its ribs formed by mountain chains, which is caught between the continents of India and China and spread out towards the Pacific. It descends from a height of over 10,000 feet to a submarine plateau so shallow that at a relatively recent geological period man could walk dryshod to Indonesia, towards which the Malay peninsula still extends its interminable length. Indochina belongs to the main land mass in the sense that its whole life flows from there, down the rivers which rise in eastern Tibet—the Red River, the Menam, the Salween, the Irrawaddy, the Mekong. The rivers meander and spread their waters ever more widely as the mountains tail off, and finally deposit their alluvium for the benefit of man. But having taken its substance from the continent, Indochina turns its back on the land, pointing seaward with its deltas which are like gateways open to the ocean. It is a funnel through which Asia's superfluity of soil and of men can be filtered out and channeled towards the distant islands of Oceania."

It was the mighty Mekong River that first attracted explorers to this Southeast Asian Eden. European vessels—including

Spanish, Portuguese, French, English, and the Dutch—were in search of treasures but more importantly seeking a trading route direct to China.

Imported goods, as well as the visual accounts reported by sailors returning from the Far East, became inspiration for designers in Europe. By the 18th century, all of Europe and the Americas were awash with a fevered desire for goods from the Orient. Inspiration and invention drove Western artisans in creating new adaptations to meet market demand. Their interpretations of Oriental products became the style that altered the taste of Europeans and Americans alike, called 'Chinoiserie'.

Dawn Jacobson writes in the book *Chinoiserie*: "Chinoiserie is an oddity. It is a wholly European style whose inspiration is entirely oriental. True chinoiseries are not pallid or incompetent imitations of Chinese objects. They are the tangible and solid realizations in the West of a land of the imagination: an exotic, remote country, fabled for its riches, that through the centuries remained cloud-wrapped, obstinately refusing to allow more than a handful of foreigners beyond its gates".

Chinoiserie represented sophistication and worldliness, appealing to aristocrats as well as ordinary folks in the West. The style flourished when respected craftsmen interpreted Chinese elements into their trade productions. The well-known cabinetmaker Thomas Chippendale in England didn't just apply these elements as decoration, he altered the very shapes and scale of his furniture while adding details such as faux-bamboo turnings and Chinese-like pierced

fretwork. Frenchman Joseph Cavoret developed wood-working methods that imitated bamboo on hardwoods; he applied for a patent in 1859 to protect his techniques. Entire rooms in elegant homes were fitted with Chinoiserie wallpapers, textiles, and furnishings. Interpretations of Chinese designs appeared in the stylized chrysanthemums, dragons, and phoenix-like birds woven into Italian brocades and silks. France and Germany studied the exquisite imported porcelains and set up production in factories such as Sevres and Meissen. Brilliant red or black Japanned lacquer finishes with gold-leafed scenes on chests and chairs became vogue. English silver tankards appeared with adapted Chinoiserie details while productions of cotton, linen, and chintz referred to motifs from China and India.

ABOVE Antique blue and white jars from the Kangxi period (early 17th century). The vase on gilt bronze base is a Blue of Hue from the Khai Dinh (1916-25) Vietnamese Emperor period. The covered vase on right is 19th century. Ceramics called 'Blue of Hue' were made in China for the Vietnamese Imperial Court in Hue. Similar styles of pottery arrived in Europe during the Golden Age of Maritime Cargo trade. Such cargoes influenced European artists in developing the style known as Chinoiserie. All pieces shown are from the collection of LIM Du Minh.

RIGHT Palladian columns merge with elements of Chinese and Vietnamese design in this Indochine architectural adaptation. The gardens continue the Indochine feeling with a variety of tropical indigenous plants combined with roses and olive trees imported from France. This home speaks eloquently of the design imagery of Southeast Asia—with a viewpoint encom-passing the beauty and devotion to harmony with nature—achieved in this home owned and designed by LIM Du Minh.

OPPOSITE An elegant sitting area in the main salon of LIM Du Minh's home, balances an inspired mix of furnishings and fine art objects dating from the 17th century.

Parisian nouveau riche of the 18th and 19th century encouraged the proliferation of the new style by commissioning artists to add amusing Chinoiserie motifs into Rococo asymmetrical scrolls and flourishes. Architectural facades, furniture, and furnishings were completely garlanded with imaginary scenes: there were gardens filled with pagodas, plum blossoms, delicate Asian ladies, and mandarins in embroidered robes traipsing over arched bridges set in exotic landscapes shared by long-tailed birds and monkeys. In 1820, near the apogee of the Chinoiserie exuberance, architect John Nash designed The Royal Pavilion at Brighton for King George IV as a pleasure palace to pamper his mistress. The exorbitance of the Royal Pavilion became synonymous with fin-de-siecle extravagance, setting a tone for change.

Indochine Style emerged toward the end of this period, in the late 19th century, when several cultural and political changes occurred simultaneously. Fragmented and war-torn Europeans were weary of lavishness and the ersatz results forced on society from the industrial revolution. Over-decoration appeared preposterous, especially in contrast with the sleek new forms that were arriving from French Indochina.

Designs from Indochina were free of applied decoration, they were appealingly natural and real in their simplicity. The furnishings made from native bamboo were genuine; they required no fret-worked details or faux-wood turnings to become other than they intrinsically 'are'. Motifs derived from the naturally occurring flora and fauna of Indochina appeared in textiles, arts, and crafts. Architectural details respected the model of 'form follows function'. By emphasizing the horizontal, overruling the vertical, a nurturing, earth-based energy is felt. Regional materials were used, honoring the organic rather than the machine made. Chinoiseries were the fancy of European artists of what Cathay might be—while Indochine Style is innately Asian, it is authentic.

Coinciding with Europe's growing fatigue of the highly decorative Rococo and Baroque embellishments and their desire for the authentic; disfavour in the social ambitions of L'Indochine française administrations was voiced from the Metropole.

Imperial France's administrative policy in the first forty years in Indochina was to reconstruct the colonies in the mirror image of France. Grand boulevards redefined city planning while governmental and residential buildings were built in the manner of European classicism. Structures with Greek columned colonnades crowned with elaborate facades encircled airless stuccoed rooms. While these forms of classic European style architecture served the governments' desire to appear authoritarian, a growing French sentiment realized their styles were tasteless, sugary confections resembling overly decorated wedding cakes compared to the intrinsic beauty and comfort of native architecture so infinitely more suited to the tropics.

The Empire's early policy of 'assimilation' was rejected at the turn of the century as economically unsound as well as politically and morally failed. Assimilation theory concluded the cultural pre-dominance of French language, education system, laws and cultural style should prevail in the colony. The other camp of colonial theorist held 'association' as a more humanistic approach that respected indigenous people and their cultural differences, including placing value on their historic monuments and offering social services.

Professor Gwendolyn Wright cites, in *The Politics of Design in French Colonial Urbanism*, two writers of the time who expressed the values of 'association':

Louis Vignon (1919), "[France pledged] its determination to pursue ever more effectively towards the colonial peoples the generous policy of 'association' which will continue to assure their progressive incorporation in the national unity". And Jules Harmond's *Dominations et colonisation* (1910), "association meant scrupulous respect for the manners, customs and religion of natives".

Using these two idealistic examples,
Wright argues: "In neither instance did
the ultimate goal revolve around cultural
benevolence; the authors were searching for
a policy that would make European economic
and political power work more effectively,
reducing the need for force". Whatever the
inclination of the French might have been in
ruling the colony in the early 1900's; native
aesthetics were incorporated into artistic
design from this time on.

Acceptance of Southeast Asian motifs
was aided by the intellectual and artistic
hostility towards in-dustrialization forcing
a trend toward simplification of arts and
lifestyle. *Revue des Arts Decoratifs* was
required reading for the design conscious
and once again, artists responded to social

needs for change with exhibitions at the Paris
World's Fair of 1900 where the French were
unrivaled in the celebration of decorative arts.
The short-lived but influential Art Nouveau
movement was a sensuous indulgence of
curvaceous subjects drawn from nature:
motifs contained female figures in long
flowing robes, twisting snakes and sea life,
climbing vines with tendrils and gossamer
dragonflies. These subjects were ordinary
themes to the Indochinese, familiar scenes
experienced daily. Dark mahogany, teak,
rosewood, and other abundant hardwoods
were materials readily available for the
capable wood carvers of French Indochina to
use in adapting their forms to the Art Nouveau
productions; or was it the Art Nouveau
artisans who drew on motifs from Indochina

that were arriving in Europe at this same time? French Impressionist painters in mid-1800's developed an artistic expression that used bright colors and candid compositions. Japonism has long been recognized as a major influence in the Impressionist style of Mary Cassatt and Henri Matisse; credit is given to the patterns of imported paper goods arriving in France from Japan. However, mid-19th century visual arts from Indochina expressed a true feeling of impressionism.

Indochine interpretations softened the edges of Chinoiserie and Art Nouveau, adding a lightness to the designs while managing to maintain the casual, unpretentious lifestyle of Indochina. The designs were instinctively fundamental, natural with sophisticated ease.

At the height of the French colonization (early to mid-20th century), the Southeast Asians were enthusiastically utilizing Art Deco and Art Moderne in their architecture, crafts, and furniture.

The natural materials and pared-down lines of Indochine Style fit international trends toward simplification of form and the elimination of ornament. The emergence of the Style occurred just when architects Ludwig Mies van der Rohe in the United States, Le Corbusier in France, and Walter Gropius in Germany were seeking to develop an architectural style with clarity and simplicity. They rejected bourgeois decorative details using principles of classical architecture in the purest of form. By the 1920's, Ludwig Mies van der Rohe had coined the phrase 'less is more' and the Bauhaus group became known as the founders of Modern Architecture, also known as International Style.

At this fortuitous time in world history Indo-china—ripe with cultural and artistic influence from India and China—was poised to meld artistic abilities with the stylish aptitude of the French. It was a moment in time when a coming together of social, political, and artistic ideas occurred with the strengths of the native Southeast Asians. Indochine Style began to influence successful designers every where to use the subtle forms and serenity of Asian designs to bring character to an otherwise dispirited pastiche.

Indochina...that mystical place idealized and promoted by the world gave birth to Indochine Style...an unmistakable and authentic style.

OPPOSITE (right) Many French colonial villas from the early 20th century in SaiGon and HaNoi are delightful examples of the Art Deco/Art Moderne architectural styles.

LEFT Credited as one of the first examples of Indochine-style architecture, architect Ernest Hébrard embodied the theory of 'association' in designing the Louis Finot Museum of the École française d'Extrême-Orient in Hanoi, 1931 (now the History Museum of Hanoi). The design integrates a broad range of Far Eastern traditions with a nod to Beaux-Arts planning.

Indochina: A History of Cultural Fusion

Indochina was created out of the fabulous East, a coming together of two great empires—India and China. The Golden Age of Greater India and The Celestial Kingdom met and melded in the luxuriant, tropical countries of Laos, Cambodia, and VietNam.

PREVIOUS PAGES *(left)* Capturing the essence of Indochine Style, this elegant colonial gate leading to the Temple of Le Thai To has neo-classic columns with Indochinese motifs in the wrought-iron work. The Temple was erected in HaNoi in 1896 to honor one of VietNam's greatest heroes, Emperor Le Thai To, also called Le Loi (Later Le dynasty—15th century). *(right)* Segment of an ancient Cham relief at MySon.

RIGHT There are floating communities throughout the maze of inlets and coves in HaLong Bay populated by people living on their boat or in a floating house. HaLong Bay is known as The Bay of the Descending Dragon, in the Gulf of Tonkin, north VietNam.

FAR RIGHT The ancient name of Laos, Lan Xang, meaning The Lands of a Million Elephants, is honored in this eave decoration on a rural colonial cottage in northern Laos. Conservation efforts by the Laos government and international groups are underway to maintain the small wild elephant population that remains.

THE COUNTRIES of Indochina unfurl like ribbons from the northern highlands to settle gently against each other, trailing down to the Mekong Delta. Threads of water flow throughout; a watery world bound together by mountainous ridges and low country deltas. These great rivers provide an abundance of sea foods, create arable floodplains for agriculture and serve as waterways for commerce. Throughout its turbulent past, the cultural traditions and the economic vagaries of Indochina are tied to the soil, the rivers, and to the sea. Once adventurers began sailing the great oceans, Indochina's extensive coastlines and river deltas were an inviting anchorage in lands that extend from the Equator to the Tropic of Cancer.

Long before the arrival of European traders, there is a recorded history of centuries of invaders to Indochina; a history of conflict and changing borders...seizure, control, loss of control, occu-pation, turmoil, and violence. The ancient names—The Lands of a Million Elephants (*Lan Xang*), the Lands of The Flying Blue Dragon (*Van Lang*), and the Lands of Mountains (*Phnom Funan*) are found in the grand imperial records of China along with extensive accounts of explorations into the regions. Remarkably, the nations of those historical names—Laos, VietNam, and Cambodia—are at last flying their individual flags of independence.

To search for the origins of Indochine Style we must consider the earliest of foreign explorers who traveled overland from India and China through Burma and Thailand. Another route came from north China by way of the Philippines and the South China Sea. China is the powerful northern neighbor curving around the top of VietNam and Laos;

the border shaped like the back of a dragon, a boundary that has changed and moved over the centuries as a dragon frolicking in the sea. It is said the Chinese moved down into Indochina, according to a Mandarin, like 'silk-worms, relentlessly nibbling on their mulberry leaves'. Northern VietNam and Laos retain many Chinese sensibilities evidenced in architectural styles, crafts, and textiles.

Influences from China in Indochina

Vietnamese dynasties fought the Chinese aggression as well as their own civil wars for the next 900 years; almost a millennium of unrest when all of life's cultural, political, and architectural arenas were deeply influenced by the Chinese. The traditional architecture of the Viet ethnic majority (there are 54 ethnic groups with the Viet representing about 88 percent of the population) developed during this time of upheaval. The Viets made adaptations to the Chinese-style pagodas, citadels, palaces, and private dwellings to suit their sense of aesthetics and accommodated available materials or local weather conditions.

Traditions of Indochina influenced by Chinese occupation are most evident in the north of VietNam where it is possible to see and feel an accumulation of history that is palpable in the population and visual in the architecture. During the 8th–3rd century BC, large migrations of poor Chinese—the Chin Emperor exiled as many as 50,000—sought relief from the tyranny of warlords. They settled into the countryside bringing along their cultural preferences for lifestyle including

the philosophies of Confucius, Lao Tzu, and Buddhism, their handi-crafts, and methods of building construction.

Concurrent with this migration in the northern provinces, a highly sophisticated Vietnamese society known as Dong Son (Bronze Age, 7th–2nd century BC) developed. From the intricate designs incised in bronze and iron implements uncovered at archeological sites, we learn the Dong Son Culture cultivated wet-rice using a series of dykes to contain floodwaters of the rivers and they built dwellings on stilts. The stilt houses had steep, curved pirogue-shaped roofs and were probably built of bamboo similar to

BELOW Until the 19th century, the only way into the walled village of HaNoi was through one of sixteen gates. O Quan Chuong is the last of these citadel gates. The ancient capital named Thang Long (Soaring Dragon), has a history of more than a thousand years. HaNoi's commuters enjoy this architectural reminder of a glorious period in VietNam's creative history.

BELOW The pagoda in Hoan Kiem Lake in Hanoi, is in commemoration of a legend dating from 1427 when Emperor Le Loi defeated Chinese troupes sent by the Ming dynasty...a victory achieved in part by his possession of a magic sword

OPPOSITE Stylized guardians stand as sentinels on the roof of this pavilion on the grounds of the Temple of Literature.

those presently seen in the Central Highlands. The Dong Son society ended when Chinese feudal rulers gained control of the northern provinces in the 2nd century BC.

From the far northern provinces of VietNam down to the central coastal areas of Hue and HoiAn, the fundamental style in temple and pagoda architecture are reminders of the heavy-timbered, post and beam construction seen in China. Tile roofs are upturned at the eaves and decorated with mystical creatures. Vivid colors of vermillion and ochre continue the familiarity with China, however on closer inspection, each

of the elements have definable attributes to Vietnamese traditions. Timber columns are elegantly shaped from one trunk (not assembled as in China) terminating on a plinth that sits upon the stylobate. Large steep roofs with low horizontal planes appear to float over the structure. Aiding this appearance of lightness are the slightly curving four corners with decorated eaves and gables. Cross-section studies of the Vietnamese construction show the roof has straight lines with only the corners curving upward; the arc of the Chinese roof is continuous, created by an intricate fit of rafters. Baked tiles are either, 'fish-scale shape', 'ying/yang shape' or tube tiles. Sculptures are characterized by simplicity of line using motifs drawn from nature. Each building has an enclosed room opening to a verandah. If the building is multi-chambered, in both large and small structures, there are an irregular number of rooms (3, 5, 7, 9, or 11). Posts and beams are locked together with timbered rafters by mortise and tenon techniques to form a solid framework that supports the steep roofs. The architecture of each dynasty is discernible by slight variations from these basic traditional elements.

By the year 1010, the great Vietnamese dynasty of King Ly Thai To had ousted Chinese rule and built the capital of his empire on the banks of the Red River. The King christened the new capital Thang Long—Soaring Dragon—a fitting name in that the dynasty of King Ly Thai To ruled over one of the most glorious periods in VietNam's history. Thang Long, renamed HaNoi, will celebrate a thousand year anniversary in 2010 as the capital of VietNam.

While the country was at peace during the reign of the Ly dynasty, its scholars, writers, and artists enjoyed an era of great creativity. In honor of the ideals of scholarly life, a place of learning was constructed: The Temple of Literature—Quoc Tu Giam (Van Mieu) the first National University of VietNam.

Temple of Literature

"In the Autumn of the year Canh Tuat, the second year of Than Vu (1070), in the 8th lunar month, during the reign of King Ly Thanh Tong, the Temple of Literature was built. The statues of Confucius, his four best disciples were carved, 71 other statues of Confucian scholars were painted. Ceremonies were dedicated to them in each of the four seasons. The Crown Princes studied here".

— *The Complete History of the Great Viet*

The brightest of students from all over the country came to Quoc Tu Giam to study the Confucian classics—including poetry, literary composition, and political administration—with famous, court-appointed mandarins. Students prepared for about three years to take national and then royal exams to become doctor laureates and mandarins. The gardens of Van Mieu are graced with stone steles, relics of the early period, that are engraved with the names and birth places of 1,307 laureates of 82 exams held between the years 1442 and 1779. Text on the stele of year 1442 advises: "Virtuous and talented men are state sustaining elements. The strength and prosperity of a state depends on its stable vitality and it becomes weaker as such vitality

ABOVE The Temple of Literature was built in the 11th century in the classical Vietnamese architectural style with roof tiles of the 'fish-scale' shape. Large timber posts sit on stone plinth that reside on the stylobate. Delicate carpentry details of the verandah balustrade adds a sense of airiness to an otherwise heavy structure.

fails. That is why all the saint emperors and clear-sighted kings didn't fail in seeing to the training of men of talent and the employment of literati to develop this vitality".

In the 19th century, a French military doctor hinted in his journal of the pomp and formality he witnessed at Van Mieu as the winners of manda-rinal examinations paraded from the countryside to receive honors for their educational achievements.

"Mandarins of the city and province, dressed in ceremonial robes, would come to meet

them. The president of the jury would then solemnly render homage to the soul of the philosopher. After the rites, everyone would sit down in the pagoda for a sumptuous feast offered by the governor."
— *Une Campagne au Tonkin* (1884–1886) by *Dr. Hocquard*

Mandarin examinations were discarded and The Temple of Literature all but forgotten with the introduction of the French colonial education system. The use of *quoc-ngu* (a Latin-based script of vernacular Vietnamese devised by Father Alexandre de Rhodes in the 17th century) became the standard for literary composition rather than Vietnamese characters.

Later, Dr. Hocquard wrote: "Numerous crow families have settled among the trees and have multiplied undisturbed under protection of the philosopher. As we approached, the birds took flight, making lugubrious noises. They have given their name to the temple, and French people living in HaNoi call it only by the name of Pagoda of Crows."

Twice each year, spring and summer during the French rule, the deserted Temple of Literature opened for ceremonial occasions for scholars and local dignitaries to pay their respects to Confucius. When the French returned to VietNam for a second occupation in 1946, the Temple of Literature became a secondary school and then an art school. Following the Indochina War of 1946–1954, revolutionaries in the new Vietnamese government ignored the Temple; it was felt the conservative nature of Confucianism was responsible for the defeat of the country in the previous century. Only after Ho Chi Minh, the much loved revolutionary leader and President of the New Republic of VietNam, made a trip into China to show respect to Confucius at his birthplace was the Temple given full reverence once again.

This treasure of ancient architecture with its extant artifacts and lovely gardens, cover many city blocks in the heart of HaNoi. The compound is being restored as it was during the Le dynasty when there were 235 classrooms, many auxiliary rooms and dormitories for 300 students.

The Chinese philosophies penetrate Vietnamese life through the abstract practice of *phong thuy* (feng-shui or geomancy). The Temple of Literature complex was sited by Ly dynasty geomancers (*thay-phap*: the geomancer, spirit medium, astrologer) to be in harmony with the nearby Taoist Bich Cau Temple and the Buddhist One Pillar Pagoda. In ancient and modern day VietNam, *phong thuy* is consulted to bring good luck and fortune when selecting auspicious days for passage-of-life events (marriage, births, deaths) or when making political or architectural decisions. A balance must be maintained between Heaven (*thien*) and Earth (*dja*), betweenn human beings (*nhan*), between male and female (ying-yang) and with the Universe through the five basic elements: water (*thuy*), fire (*hoa*), wood (*moc*), metal

ABOVE The center door of the main entry gate into the Temple of Literature was reserved for the king of the mandarins. The other doors were used by ordinary people who came to study or worship in the temple. The gateway is decorated with dragons, lion dogs, and the phoenix. Confucius said: "The Superior Man seeks within himself. The Inferior Man seeks within others". Gardens and pathways within the Temple of Literature grounds offer abundant opportunities to stop, study and contemplate works of art while seeking within oneself."

RIGHT A red lacquered and gold leaf altar with a statue of Confucius in the Temple of Literature in HaNoi. The heavy timbered construction of this classic building is lightened by the playful details of the balustrade railings and the balusters.

(*kim*), and earth (*tho*). The geomantic compass *la kinh* is consulted today as it was in the past, utilizing philosophies of 'Five Happiness' (longevity, wealth, health, virtuousness, and a peaceful end). Decorative motifs are crafted in wood, terracotta, stone, and metal to represent the elements. Chrysanthemum, willow, apricot, and lotus are used as symbols of the four seasons and there are usually sculptures or paintings of the four sacred animals—dragon, griffin, turtle, and phoenix. The peace and beauty of the gardens surrounding the Temple of Literature in HaNoi illustrate all of these principles.

During the same time China was invading the north of VietNam, ocean-going merchant ships from India were sailing north, trading throughout the Indonesian islands and on to the South China Sea. They surely crossed the wake of the Chinese as they voyaged up the coasts of Indochina, into the expansive deltas and then inland up the many magnificent rivers of Cambodia bringing with them knowledge about new religions, customs, and artistic skills.

ABOVE **In the Temple of Literature, intricate roof support elements allow a visual expansion of space from one room to the next, juxtaposing large-scale timber construction and delicate design. It is an architectural delight for the eyes, while allowing the flow of air in a humid climate.**

Influences from India in Indochina

Ethnohistorians and archeologists believe Indian traders and traveling Brahmins (the learned caste of India) visited Cambodia and southern VietNam during the first millennium BC. Cambodian royal courts received the travelers and learned of their society and their cultural ideas including the religious principles of Hinduism. Animistic beliefs of the native people fit neatly with the precepts of Hinduism accepting the worship of Shiva and Vishnu as supreme gods and the pantheon of spirits. The nascent societies grew out of these interactions, adopting the Hindu religion, arts, and craftsmanship to grow into the highly sophisticated cultures known as The Khmer Civilization in Cambodia and the Cham Civilization in central and south VietNam.

While the recorded history of VietNam goes back more than 2,500 years, there is little written history of Laos and Cambodia other than in Chinese Imperial records (100 AD) describing visits by Chinese ambassadors to lands they named Funan, where legends hold an Indian Brahmin called Kambu established a peaceful settlement of Indian traders. Part of the lands of Funan (a Khmer word—*phnom*) and later Chenla, became the Khmer Empire in Cambodia. By the 6th century, Funan was described as a prosperous society practicing mostly Hinduism and Mahayana Buddhism, headed by a powerful king who lived in an ornate palace, who owned many slaves and elephants. The Chinese described the buildings there as mostly made of wood.

OPPOSITE Small bricks were loose-laid to construct towers built by the Cham civilization at MySon near DaNang in VietNam. There are many stone carvings set into alcoves and niches at MySon.

TOP LEFT A soft sandstone carving in bas-relief of a dancing Shiva reflects the strong Indian influence.

BOTTOM LEFT This mystical elephant-lion is included in the vast collection of original sculpture exhibited at MySon.

OPPOSITE Cham Towers at MySon are the most impressive grouping of extant Champa architecture. Their spire-shaped shrines, *kalan*, are considered to be dwelling places for the gods rather than places used to assemble for worship

TOP LEFT An exhibition of Cham sculpture and fragments collected at MySon are exhibited inside one of the *kalan*. The art work and the structures indicate a highly sophisticated culture influenced by Hinduism from India.

BOTTOM LEFT Many fragments of stone steles found at MySon reveal information on the Cham civilization. Old Chinese trade documents list a kingdom called Lin Yi on the coast of Annam as early as the 2nd century. By the 4th century, this kingdom had become the Champa settlement situated around DaNang. At the height of the Champa civilization, there were as many as 2.5 million inhabitants.

MySon

VietNam's vestige of Indianised societies is preserved at several sites in the form of towers with the Cham Towers at MySon (near DaNang) being the most impressive grouping of extant Cham architecture. Their spire-shaped shrines, *kalan*, are considered to be dwelling places for the gods rather than places used to assemble for worship. Originally built of wood in the 4th century, the MySon complex was destroyed by fire in the 6th century then reconstructed using brick and stone. Vietnamese dynastic feuds, Chinese invasions, and the Khmer enemy in the south finally drove the Cham Kingdom of some 2.5 million people into a decline beginning in the 13th century. MySon was rediscovered for the Western world in 1889 by Frenchmen Camille Paris and Henri Parmentier, who completed an extensive documentation of all buildings. Restoration programs are ongoing following the work of a team of Polish archeologist that began towards the end of the 20th century.

ANGKOR WAT

The Khmer architectural treasure, Angkor Wat, is considered one of the world's most extensive religious monuments. A prime example of Indian influence, Angkor Wat consists of vast brick and stone temple sites (spread over more than 64 km in Cambodia) with the earliest parts of the Wat dating from the 1st century BC

The mere size of the complex is beyond imagination, but it is the craftsmanship of the masonry and the exquisite beauty of the statuary that is astonishing. The magnificence of Angkor Wat has been the subject of study from early explorers to archeologists today. In 1860, Frenchman Henri Mouhot visited Angkor after traveling for three years in Thailand, Laos, and Cambodia. Upon arriving in Battambang, a French missionary told him there were rumors of ancient ruins near the fresh water lake, the Tonle Sap. Traveling by canoe and on foot, Mouhot's party found an immense stone building with five spire-shaped towers. It was the Temple of Angkor with its towers representing the five peaks of Mount Meru.

"Mouhot did not know that he was looking at the largest religious monument in the world. He racked his imagination for comparisons in Western civilizations. Angkor Wat, he wrote later, was 'a rival to [the Temple] of Solomon and erected by some ancient Michlangelo...It is grander than anything left to us by Greece or Rome, and presents a sad contrast to the state of barbarism in which the nation is now plunged'."
   —*Angkor: The Hidden Glories*
      by Michael Freeman & Roger Warner

Mouhot's superb sketches detailed the extensive bas-reliefs of Angkor Wat and his journals suggest emotion he must have felt on the view he describes from the hill-top temple Phnom Bakheng just north of Angkor Wat: "On the one side you gaze upon the wooded plain and the pyramidal temple of Ongcor [Angkor Wat], with its rich colonnades....[in another direction] the new city, the view losing itself in the waters of the great lake on the horizon. On the opposite side stretches the long chain of mountains whose quarries, they say, furnished the beautiful stone used for the temples; and amid thick forests, which extend along the base, is the pretty, small lake which looks like a blue ribbon on a carpet of verdure...."

This journal entry is from Milton Osborn's book Mekong; followed by Osborn's own recollections of hearing writer Somerset Maugham describe Angkor Wat: "When he visited Cambodia in 1959—his second visit, for he had been there in the 1920s—the novelist Somerset Maugham followed the well-established path that led tourists to the imposing temple ruins of Angkor at their site close to the kingdom's Great Lake. Returning to Phnom Penh, and before a gathering of the English-speaking community that hung on his every word, I heard him hand down his verdict. 'No one,' he said with trembling jaw, 'no one should die before they see Angkor'."

BELOW The Pagoda Bridge in HoiAn was built during the golden era of maritime trade by the Japanese over three years beginning in 1593, from the year of the monkey to that of the dog...hence statues of each stand guard at either end. The village called Faifo was occupied by Japanese, Chinese, and Vietnamese merchants and then the French. The bridge was at one time a courthouse where conflicts between different communities were settled.

ABOVE Outdoor dining area at the Brother's Café has an unobstructed view of the Thu Bon River; once filled with tall-masted schooners sailing into Faifo from international ports. Now the river traffic is limited to local fishermen as they head out to work on the South China Sea.

OPPOSITE Rooms of the dining-bar at the Brother's Café open to the front sidewalk and onto paths leading back to the river. The original small rooms of the villa have been joined by way of arched openings, making an airy space of inviting proportions.

Cultural Fusion in Indochina

Commanders, rogues, and opportunists of every ilk were drawn to Indochina, undaunted by treacherous, uncharted travel throughout the Indonesian Archipelago, up along the coast of Indochina through the blue waters of the South China Sea. For more than 200 years, beginning in the 16th century, ships from all over the world sailed into the harbour of Faifo establishing a central port city for merchants from India, China, Portugal, Holland, England, France, and Japan.

The village of Faifo, now called HoiAn, is situated almost in the middle of the lengthy South China Sea coastline of VietNam. Long and narrow, VietNam is commonly said to resemble a shoulder yoke with baskets on either end...to the north is the basket of the

OPPOSITE Lush tropical garden with the river flowing by brings fresh breezes to cool humid afternoons in this elegant dining place... how delightful this setting to enjoy fresh Vietnamese spring rolls with a soft, translucent rice paper wrapper (*banh cuon*) and a tropical fruit smoothie.

LEFT French villas were built with large openings to help ventilate interior rooms. High ceilings allowed hot air to rise above the living area and wide verandahs shielded rooms from the hot tropical sun.

ABOVE **Shaded and cool garden courtyard welcomes visitors to HaAn Hotel. To the right is café dining offering breakfast of croissant, fresh fruits such as papaya, dragon fruit, star fruit, pomelo, or the traditional *pho*, the soup of VietNam. The white building behind the blooming bougainvillea, is the reception, office and a few guest rooms. The Bui family live upstairs.**

built fine dwellings in their cultural style, often combining a shop for business, a warehouse for merchandise and living quarters all in one location. Faifo's importance declined when the centers of trade shifted to the Gulf of Tonkin in the north or SaiGon in the south.

The once crowded River Thu Bon is now the venue for local fisherman and cottage shipbuilding companies in the peaceful village renamed HoiAn. Declared a World Heritage Site by UNESCO in 1999, HoiAn has more than 840 buildings designated as having historic importance from the period of maritime trade. The ancient facades are undergoing restoration in an active and ongoing program to preserve the unique architectural atmosphere in peaceful and quiet HoiAn.

Phan Boi Chau was the main thoroughfare of the old French quarter section of HoiAn, running parallel with the River Thu Bon. On the river-side of the street, villas were strategically positioned for shipping commerce at their back door. Now these villas are undergoing restoration, as at the Brother's Café, 27 Phan Boi Chau Street. The villa was originally home and offices of a French family until the mid-1900s when the buildings became an ice-house supplying ice to the village and to fishermen. The Indochine ambience has been completely restored in the colonial buildings, now a most romantic restaurant offering delicious regional foods along with nostalgia for days past.

Walking past Brother's Café, further down quiet Phan Boi Chau Street, there is a feeling of olden times: a sense of commerce that must have transpired in the narrow alleyways

Red River delta and on the southern end the basket of the Mekong delta. Two baskets brimming with produce from the fertile lands of these great river deltas with the ancient village Faifo balanced on the shoulder, the mid-point, of the long bamboo pole of VietNam.

With an important river of its own, the River Thu Bon, Faifo became a bustling port-of-call providing extended anchorage for safe harbor while vessels waited out the caprice of seasonal trade winds and the deluge of monsoons. Volumes of trade warranted foreign merchants to set-up permanent places of business. Silks, lacquerware, porcelain, tea, and spices were among commodities traded by the Chinese, French, Japanese, and Vietnamese storekeepers who sorted themselves out into districts. They

LEFT Graceful lines of the guest-room wing are influenced by colonial French architecture.

ABOVE Verandah railings are a compatible mix of colonial details with the wood detailing of VietNam. Louvered wood doors are closed at night for quiet and for privacy. Yin-yang tiles are the traditional roofing tile in the country.

leading back to the river's edge; children are still playing games marked with chalk on the street in front of their homes or family shop; there are no cars on Boi Chau Street, only *cyclos* (pedi-cab), bicycles, and a few motorbikes and then as the end of the street is near, there is an enticingly beautiful villa surrounded by a wall, the property of HaAn Hotel. HoiAn native, architect Bui Kien Quoc, lived in the South of France since the mid-1940's but recently returned to his hometown with the intention of having a simple place on the river. "HoiAn is a small and peaceful place and we decided to build a fisherman-type house at the river-side, a place to take tea and do nothing. From this first idea, little by little our planning grew to a villa and then to the HaAn Hotel. The energy in VietNam is very strong, an unknowable energy that seems to take over". When architect Bui Quoc found a large plot of land for sale on Phan Boi Chau Street, he knew immediately it was to be the site for their family home. He designed a villa that is really "like two houses with another space between" based on the concept of a space large enough "where we can be a lot of people living together with peaceful relations—an independence of activities". Two sets of stairs in the main villa allow freedom of movement, either from the personal family wing or from the wing for friends, family, and guests. He determined all rooms would be overlooking the courtyard. After building the villa, people of HoiAn began to ask what his intention might be with such a large home, asking if it is to be a hotel. No, that really wasn't the intention, however the town kept offering a license to open a hotel (a license

that was hard to obtain at the time) for they couldn't conceive of a family home being so large. Architect Quoc thought "why not" and designed a wing of guest rooms separate from the main villa but also overlooking the courtyard. The design concept was for this wing, set perpendicular to the villa, to resemble a street-scene of HoiAn with each set of rooms appearing to be a single, two-story house with connecting verandahs. The whole plan comes together in a most pleasing combination of HoiAn colonial French architecture along with elements in the main villa touching on the feel of Asia.

Architect Quoc remembers the colors of HoiAn, "it was the most beautiful village of every shade of blues and yellow. White was the traditional color reserved for businesses however residential renovations are ignoring the custom by using white. He feels it a mistake to forget the colors of old HoiAn, therefore at Hotel HaAn, the main villa containing the reception and office is painted white. The guest wing is painted with shades of blues and yellows in keeping with old HoiAn streetscapes of homes.

Influences from France in Indochina

French Catholic missionaries booked passage on those early sailing ships to Indochina with intention of establishing missions. Jesuit Alexandre de Rhodes first arrived in Cochin China—about 1619, then traveled to the newly established mission in HaNoi where he spent ten years with the Court of Trinh Tung and Trinh Trang. By the late 1600's, Catholicism had grown remarkably in a predominantly

ABOVE A classic wood house in Luang Prabang is built with the living space above and the space below left open to allow air flow. The lower space in this modern economy provides an area to dry newly dyed textiles.

Buddhist Indochina—an estimated 800,000 Catholics in VietNam alone.

Before Father de Rhodes left VietNam in 1630 (expelled by Trinh Trang who had become concerned due the dangers posed by the Catholic religion) he published a Vietnamese-Latin-Portuguese dictionary that lead to the development of a Romanised version of vernacular Vietnamese named *quoc-ngu*. This lasting legacy of his years in VietNam was assured when *quoc-ngu* became the official language of the Indochinese government in 1910.

France wanted a colony in the Far East to gain a competitive edge over the expanding British Empire in Hong Kong and Singapore, but the persecution of Catholics was the sanctimonious excuse. As Nicola Cooper relates in the book *France in Indochina: "French intervention in Indochina was born of religious evangelism and pursued through a combination of international imperial and maritime rivalry"*

Hoping to assure French subjects the right to trade and establish commercial bases, missionary to VietNam Archbishop Adran Pigneau de Behaine went to Versailles in 1786 to obtain approval from Louis XVI for military support for the Court of Nguyen Anh to lead an offensive against warring Vietnamese.

The King agreed to provide four ships, 1,650 men, and supplies in exchange for Nguyen Anh's promise to cede the port at DaNang and the island of Poulo Condore to France. When Louis XVI reneged on his promises, Pigneau de Behaine raised funds from French merchants in India and sailed back to VietNam with two ships manned by deserters from the French Navy. With this support, Nguyen Anh proceeded to capture control of the Cochin China delta, Hue, and Tonkin. In the following years, the Archbishop helped supply Nguyen Anh with ships, arms, and advisers to build forts, shipyards, and provide instruction in the manufacture and use of modern armaments. In 1802, Nguyen Anh became Gia Long, Emperor of VietNam.

The revolutionary period diverted France from Southeast Asia until 1820 when Gia Long's successor, Minh Mang of the Nguyen dynasty, ascended the throne. Although France had supported the Nguyen dynasty in the past, Minh Mang disliked the *prêtres étrangers* (foreign priests) in VietNam and began extensive persecution of missionaries in Indochina until the end of his reign in 1840. France's seething rivalry with the British was ignited when Great Britain gained control of Hong Kong in 1842. This move by Great Britain and the maltreatment of Catholics in VietNam served as a timely pretext for France to take control of Indochina.

France seized Indochina at a time the entire region was in a weakened condition following centuries of turbulent border wars and dynasty conflicts. Upon assuming authority in the south, Cochin China became a French colony in 1862 and Cambodia

became a protectorate when France first took possession of the Mekong delta; however they soon realized access to China was not possible via the Mekong River. To secure their holdings, France saw control over the areas bordering on China as an absolute necessity. France captured HaNoi, including the Red River delta and the entire Tonkin region in 1885. With these actions, the basins of two great rivers (the Mekong and the Red River) whose waters rise in China, had become the province of the French. This era of expansion of the French Empire into Southeast Asia created the Indochinese Union—a union colonizing Cochin China, Annam, Tonkin (VietNam in modern history), Laos, and Cambodia. Once France gained power over the entire region, they set about reorganizing the colony to a more European way of life.

"My Mother sometimes tells me that never in my whole life shall I ever again see rivers as beautiful and big and wild as these, the

ABOVE **Terraced fields of small crops step up the riverbank of the Mekong near Luang Prabang, Laos. Further down river at Vientiane, timely plantings of assorted food crops alternate with seasonal flooding on the wide alluvial plains along the Mekong.**

Mekong and its tributaries going down to the sea, the great regions of water soon to disappear into the caves of the ocean. In the surround flatness stretching as far as the eye can see, the rivers flow as if the earth sloped downwards."
—*The Lover* by Marguerite Duras

Architectural history is recorded along the banks of the great Mekong delta and up the reaches of the Mekong River where there is vernacular architecture mingled with French colonial structures. A pre-French, native architectural style is described in the 1819-20 journal of U.S. Navy Lieutenant John White titled *A Voyage to Cochinchina*. He writes of sailing up the Mekong to the small village of SaiGon where he saw housing "principally of wood, thatched with palm leaves or rice straw and one story. Some few are of brick and covered with tiles". SaiGon was razed by fire during the invasion of France in 1859 leaving a few wood dwellings.

Early commerce on the Mekong River flowed past SaiGon, through Cambodia to the upper regions of Laos. Just beyond Luang Prabang passage is largely blocked to river traffic by waterfalls. The magnificent Mekong, the world's 12th largest river, actually begins its course in Tibet, carving a sharp descent through the compact mountains and steep ravines of Northern Laos, making its way down to the South China Sea. The village of Luang Prabang straddles a peninsular that is formed by a smaller river, the Nam Khan, when it meets the huge Mekong.

Narrow passes of the Mekong open to alluvial planes near Luang Prabang. Typical Lao and Cambodian wooden houses along the river are built on stilts that rest on brick foundations—a proven structural solution for marshy lands prone to monsoonal flooding. The ground floor space between the stilts is used for working, socializing and sheltering animals. The open design also keeps the house cool, allowing breezes to flow through, helping to clear the sultriness of high humidity. There is an intricate drainage system that was in use before the French arrived—rain gutters lead from houses to ponds to help shed the volumes of rainwater in the monsoon seasons. There are more than 200 of these ponds in Luang Prabang.

Luang Prabang was placed on the UNESCO World Heritage List in 1995. The citation read: "Luang Prabang is an outstanding example of the fusion of traditional architecture and Lao urban structures with those built by European colonial authorities in the 19th and 20th centuries."

Among the many historic homes in Luang Prabang is the home of Francis Engelmann who lives full-time in Laos, devoting his time to heritage conservation and art. This classic colonial house was built in 1925 by a French aristocrat. A few years later, a Chinese merchant became the second owner after marrying a Laotian woman.

During the French Colonial times the combi-nation of wooden structure and masonry was fairly common. Mr. Engelmann told us of his home: "The house is really a combination of French ideas in the stucco below with pure Laotian-style wooden house above. The French thought wood houses were only for poor peasants, however people

OPPOSITE *(left)* The home of Francis Engelmann in Luang Prabang, Laos, is a classic colonial house built in 1925. The wide-board floors, wooden louvred doors, and period furniture in the sitting room are original in every detail. *(top right)* Rooms on the upper floor open out to the verandah allowing the flow of light and cooling breezes. *(bottom right)* A museum quality textile from the looms of Carole Cassidy's Laos Textiles, in the home of Mr. Engelmann.

ABOVE The lower floor constructed of stucco is a French concept while the second floor is a Laotian-style wooden house. The wooden houses are more comfortable in the hot, humid climate of Laos; therefore the upper floor is designated for living and sleeping.

RIGHT Entry gate to the grounds of the most famous temple in Laos, Vat Xieng Thong. The temple was built in 1560 and underwent major restoration in 1928 following King Sisavang Vong's request for funds from the French government.

BOTTOM LEFT & RIGHT Glass mosaics set on red lacquer walls at Vat Xieng Thong detail scenes of everyday life in Laos.

OPPOSITE The main sanctuary, the *sim*, at Vat Xieng Thong has a graceful three-tiered roof covering three bays. The floor plan has two aisles and three naves. During each renovation, artists were instructed to accurately restore the murals as originally designed to maintain the continuity of the spirituality of the Vat.

liked to sleep upstairs in a wood house for its coolness and lack of humidity. Even the Palace in Luang Prabang was of wood; however the French magistrates thought this inappropriate for a Royal Family and built for King Sisavang Vong a new palace using brick and stucco construction. For many years, the King continued to live in his wooden house and used the new palace only for state affairs. Laos no longer has a king, however the palace is now The Royal Palace Museum. The French brought craftsmen from VietNam who were knowledgeable in building masonry structures so that the colonial architecture in Luang Prabang is an amazing blending of French, Lao, Vietnamese, and sometimes Chinese ideas".

Mr. Engelmann uses the lower area of the house for social events and to hold salons to introduce new artists. Doors and windows of the sitting room and master bedroom suite on the second floor open to the verandah. The kitchen is built to the side of the main house at a mid-level, has a roof but open-walls. This is the traditional placement of the kitchen in houses of this period.

OPPOSITE Opposite An early Colonial/Laotian house on the main street in Luang Prabang, is lovingly restored by owner Ivan Scholte. The design and furnishings of this old house reflect the style now referred to as East-West fusion... yet here it is during the French Colonial period. This is the sleeping pavilion of Ivan Sholte's property.

TOP LEFT School girls, wearing Laotian sarong uniforms called *sin*, cycle past traditional and colonial buildings on the main street of Luang Prabang.

BOTTOM LEFT The sleeping house (see interior view opposite) is the smaller structure connected via a breezeway to the larger living quarters on the right.

The decorations and the architectural design of the entry gate to a Pagoda (a Buddhist temple) in HaNoi are strongly influenced by Chinese features.

The day we visited Mr. Engelmann, tea was served on the verandah as morning light dappled over the worn wood floors, then played into adjoining rooms along with a soft breeze that gently cooled the air. We watched the comings and goings of the neighborhood from our treehouse-like vantage while sipping delicious tea and experiencing the genteel atmosphere of living in an antique wooden house in Luang Prabang.

Just around the block from Francis Engelmann's house, half hidden behind old mango trees, is the Vat Nong Monastery. Twice each day the old monastery resounds with bells and drums marking the time for prayers and meditation for the Buddhist monks and initiates. Luang Prabang is a village of historic temples, and of the 66 erected before the French colonial period, 32 remain. Wat Xieng Thong and Wat Mai Suwannaphumaham date from around the 15th century.

Perched at the northern end of the peninsula overlooking the Mekong is the very beautiful and artistically decorated Vat Xieng Thong. The wat was built in the year 1560 by King Setthathirat and remained under royal patronage until 1975. The *sim* (ordination hall—called *sim* after the sima stone sacred tablets), is a classic example of Luang Prabang style temple architecture. The monastery grounds have an astounding array of small temples with walls covered in mosaic tiles and mirrors as well as several *stupas*.

In contrast to the early architecture of Laos, the wood structures of VietNam feature huge timbers in post-and-beam construction, with a handsome system of exposed trusses. In the Old Quarter of HaNoi, each street is a

veritable museum of structures dating from the mid-1700s, reflecting a Chinese influence mellowed by the aesthetic refinement of the cultured Vietnamese. HaNoi remains the capital of VietNam but from 1888 to 1945 it was the capital of Indochina, a period of time that is caught—if somewhat crumbling—in the fantastically detailed facades of HaNoi French architecture.

Colonial buildings constructed during this period stand side-by-side with ancient Vietnamese structures. The Old Quarter is an area of guilds or craftsmen. At one time there were 36 guilds and 36 streets each street specialized in the merchandise of a single craft or product. The name of the street told the story: such as Ma May Street sold rattan, Thuoc Bac sold herbal medicines, Hang Than for charcoal, or Hang Ga for chicken. Cha Ca Street was and still is the place to go for roasted fish and the Hanoian fish dish, *cha ca*—morsels of white fish dusted with turmeric are fried tableside in oil, then served up with fresh cilantro, scallions, basil, peanuts, fresh dill, lime wedges, and chili sauce along with rice vermicelli—so tasty! As is the 104-year old structure housing the restaurant Cha Ca La Vong.

Inhabitants of the Old Quarter began to move away as the guild concept is impacted by modern HaNoi. Now there are a total of about 50 streets in the area and a street may have mixed businesses springing up amidst the guild; but the Old Quarter remains a labyrinth of narrow streets turning into alleys turning back to lanes, twisting and turning so that one can easily lose direction and mill about. Finding ones' way out of the Old

Quarter will land you back into the wide boulevards preferred by French city planners.

Tube houses are a traditional style of building seen in the Old Quarter...named from the shape (one-room about 3-5 meters wide with several consecutive rooms, 20-60 meters deep). To gain access from front to back of the tube house, it is necessary to pass through the consecutive rooms. Open courtyards separate rooms, allowing the penetration of air and light. Transaction of the family business occurs in the first floor space that opens directly onto the street; family quarters are to the back or on the second or upper floors above the business. The preserved historical house at 87 Ma May offers a look back into history and the way of living and working in a classic tube house.

OPPOSITE Light streams into the open courtyard of this historic tube house in the old quarter of HaNoi. Looking toward the street, the first room would be for the shop. Vietnamese platform tables and stools provide an area to offer clients a cup of green tea before transacting business.

ABOVE The kitchen is at the rear of the tube house and has an open courtyard with a well. A closed room for the toilet is off this back courtyard.

LEFT Front room of the upper floor contains the ancestral altar and seating to socialize with friends, often used by the men. Family living quarters are at the rear.

TOP RIGHT Thuy An's tailoring business is located in a classic tube house that stands between other French colonial buildings in HaNoi's Old Quarter. The family garden on the upper balcony is filled with orchids, tended by Thuy An's husband, Mr. Bin Manh Tien.

BOTTOM RIGHT The family sitting room on the second floor above the shop is artfully decorated with a fine collection of Vietnamese art objects. The open design of the tiles set in the walls above windows and the doors opening onto the street-side balcony provide ventilation.

BOTTOM LEFT A vitrine displays antique Vietnamese blue ware. The gold leaf wood carvings on top of the cabinet are decorative pieces used for ritual occasions.

Thuy An Fashion Design shop in HaNoi's Old Quarter is a contemporary business operating in a restored traditional tube house with a few additions from French colonial times. Thuy An designs clothing, takes custom orders, and runs her business on the street level of this ancient house on Pho Hang Bong, one of the 36 guild streets, (the name means 'street selling cotton merchandise') now a street of tailors selling cotton and silk. Thuy An and her husband, Mr. Bin Manh Tien, have restored their tube house to its original beauty and are raising their two boys here.

LEFT Thuy An conducts her tailoring business on the first floor. The third-floor room with balcony is the family temple area. The second-floor, under the family temple room is additional space for the shop and offices and behind the offices are family quarters. An original skylight in the third floor ceiling floods the lower floors with natural light.

ABOVE This Vietnamese carved table displays part of the family collection of fine objects. The jar of coins was excavated from a site in northern VietNam near the border of Quangzi province in China; dating from the time of VietNam's 8th Emperor Han Nghi, c. AD41.

ABOVE An antique timbered hall house was dismantled from its original site in northern VietNam and reassembled at the Moon River Resort.

TOP RIGHT Restored old gate at Moon River is used to devise a focal point to this walled garden path.

BOTTOM RIGHT Statuary in the gardens of Moon River set a light-hearted feeling.

OPPOSITE A new structure at Moon River borrows elements of traditional Vietnamese/ Chinese architecture... the roof tiles are laid in the fish-scale pattern, wooden doors have latticed openings, and the circle window displays the stylized characters of longevity.

On the banks of the Duong River, in the Red River delta, lies an innovative retreat, the Moon River Complex. Not far from HaNoi, Moon River features an innovative mix of traditional and modern Asian architecture. This sanctuary offers a place to rejuvenate, enjoy fine dining while watching the ever changing scenes of river commerce, and the experience of staying in a century–old Vietnamese timber house. Mortise and tenon post and beam constructions allowed the old houses to be disassembled and moved to be reassembled in the same plan. Antique timber houses were moved from a northern province in VietNam to the Moon River site to be used as guest rooms and an antique community building for large gatherings.

RIGHT Many restaurants in VietNam, as the Quon An Ngoc restaurant in SaiGon, serve traditional Vietnamese foods accompanied by *pain baguette français*.

OPPOSITE The Paris Deli in the Old Quarter, HaNoi.

France settled into Indochina and began massive programs of change and reorganization that impacted the entire region through education, commerce, arts, and architecture, including town planning. Major cities were changed to echo France's love of boulevards lined with trees and grand buildings, abundant parks, luxurious villas, and stately public buildings. There was an enormous disparity of wealth and comfort between the colonizers and the natives resulting in a period of French history that repeats a familiar and far too common story of conquering countries dehumanizing native citizens while exploiting natural resources. Yet it is considered by many that it was the French who were colonized.

Toward the end of the occupation, the style of the native people had gained appeal to the French; they found a certain pleasure in the Indochine way of life they had developed there ex post facto. Collaborations occurred not only in the arts or social forms, but in the cuisine as well. Exotic tropical foods, new and exciting to French palates are used in a myriad of dishes imprinted with French methods of cooking. La belle France is revealed in the Southeast Asian's preference for strong morning coffee, rather than tea as in most Far Eastern countries, and street vendors sell warm baguettes. Al fresco dining is de rigueur reflecting the traditional French café society.

France pulled out of Indochina in 1954, a colonization that lasted close to a century. Their accomplishments include: thousands of kilometers of roadways useable in all seasons; they did not build hospitals but helped ameliorate disease through vaccination programs, clean water, and sanitation schemes; they built libraries and published classic books in affordable editions. And then there is the delicious bread and coffee! Older people in these countries speak French and many hold the French in nostalgic affection. The French imprint on Indochina wears a sophisticated patina of age, like a fine old painting where the lacquer has gone a bit yellow lending a mellow haze that softens the view and refines a romanticized dream of a place.

The people of Indochina have persevered against foreign nations with far greater power than their own. Laos, Cambodia, and VietNam now have their national sovereignty and have maintained much of their cultural heritage while celebrating the best France left behind. While acknowledging the history of cultural fusion, the populations are energized with newly found freedoms and their cities are being revitalized.

Vividly colored ceramic tile decorations along with the bracketed roof and tile vents beneath the overhangs add Indochine styling to this French villa in SaiGon. The old villa has been completely renovated to become the Nam Phan gourmet restaurant. (right) The 1920s Majestic Hotel still overlooks the SaiGon River at Number One Duan Dong Khoi, the fashionable street previously known as Rue de Catinat.

A Romance with Indochina: French Colonial Rule

*Nostalgia for Indochina: those who have not experienced it
cannot understand its bewitchment.*

—Les Asiates, *by Jean Hougron*

OPPOSITE LEFT Baskets of steamed rice, Vietnamese fresh vegetables, and bowls of ingredients for the national soup specialty, *pho*, are accompanied by warm *pain baguette Français*.

OPPOSITE RIGHT Merchandise of every description is offered in Cho Binh Tay located in ChoLon, the old Chinese district of Ho Chi Minh City. Each day, a steady stream of buyers, traders, and porters pass under the handsome clock tower to transact business in this vast emporium. Designed during colonial times by a French architect for a wealthy Chinese merchant, this historic market represents the coming together of cultural styles in Indochina: the double-tiered, long and low roof lines of the richly colored ochre building is classic Vietnamese architecture decorated with Chinese elements.

SAIGON, HaNoi, DaLat, Phnom Phen, Luang Prabang, Vientiane... The very names of Indochina's cities kindles excitement in the imaginations of romantics everywhere. These distant cities conjure visions of daring adventure with unknown possibi-lities: idealized fantasies of thrilling, mysterious journeys—a longboat puttering down the Mekong dropping anchor in remote villages or perhaps a steamship passage through ethereal HaLong Bay. Actual reports of those having visited Indochina clearly describe the beauty of the landscape and the people but more difficult to describe is something of far greater impact...it has been said: "It is not about the beauty of the landscape or its people, which it has, nor about any one particular thing but about that ineffable 'feeling' one takes away and is never forgotten." There is a lingering romance with Indochina.

Contemporary films have enriched the fan-tasies, providing visual stimulus to novels of the period. Jean Hougron's *Les Asiates* or Marguerite Duras' *The Lover*, and of course Graham Greene's *The Quiet American*, have all contributed to imaginary characterizations. Set decorations in *The Scent of Green Papaya* form a retrospective exhibiting the beauty of Indochine interiors. Film director Jean-Jacque Annaud was so moved by his experiences after visiting VietNam before filming *The Lover* (adapted from the Duras novel of the same title) wrote in an essay, Impressions of VietNam: "I was on a quest for the emotions I had felt when reading *The Lover*. Marguerite Duras had plunged me into Asia. The pages smelled of jasmine, charcoal fire, and incense. With her I crossed the breathtaking immensity of the Mekong, I wandered the flatness of the delta's rice paddies that run as far as the eyes can see. I followed the rosewood-hatted young girl that she had been along the wide, tree-shaded avenues of the colonial city. I ambled beside the gardens overflowing with flowers, caught glimpses of the villas with their verandas in the white part of town. I accompanied her up to the haughty French High School building. Then I lost her in the red-and-gold exuberance of the Chinese part of town. And at dusk, in the silent solitude of the dorm, with her I heard, carried over on the wind from the lagoon, the faraway singing of a beggar-woman.

Ho Chi Minh City (SaiGon)

Vietnamese settled the hamlet of Prey Nokor, Cambodia in the 16th Century; annexing the lands for south VietNam and changing the name to SaiGon; meaning *kapok* forest or cotton flower from the translation of the Khmer words *prey kor*.

The small colony of SaiGon became the capital of Cochin China after 2,000 French soldiers and eight warships sailed up the SaiGon River in 1859 and successfully took control. A Vietnamese counter-attack waged from the backs of elephants failed, but before fleeing with most of the 200,000 Saigonese, all rice stores were burned along with most of the village. SaiGon soon grew to a sophisticated ville Française with the building of prestigious administrative offices and other buildings including stately villas for the new émigré from France. New structures were highly ornamented in the manner of European Classic Baroque, a style thought to be representative of French superiority deserving of the name Paris de l'Extreme-Orient.

SaiGon was renamed Ho Chi Minh City (H.C.M.C.) following the reunification of the country in 1975, however, residents still fondly refer to their city by its old name. There are many districts within the area of H.C.M.C. including: SaiGon, the district mainly occupied by the French, and the district Cho Lon that is home to resident Chinese and where the market Cho Binh Tay daily offers an unfathomable variety of merchandise.

RIGHT One could say the pièce de résistance of French colonial architecture and Baroque decoration might be this 'crème puff' of a building built in 1901-08 as Hotel deVille in SaiGon. It is now the headquarters of the People's Committee of the Socialist Republic of VietNam on Nguyen Hue Street, formerly du Boulevard Charner.

BELOW LEFT A public building from French Colonial era in SaiGon glows in the bright tropical sun. The banner, *Chuc mung nam moi*—Happy New Year, is displayed during the Tet celebrations.

BELOW RIGHT The courtyard of Le Quy Don; a boarding school located in the French section of SaiGon is referenced in Marquerite Duras' auto-biographical novel, *The Lover*.

OPPOSITE The Town Theatre (1899) and the Continental Hotel (1880) are in the heart of SaiGon on Dong Khoi street. The Continental Hotel was used as a venue in several films including Indochine and The Quiet American.

Nam Phan Restaurant in District One of old SaiGon is an inspiring renovation accomplished by the KhaiSilk Corporation who are noted for fine restaurants serving traditional food with a gourmet touch. With the cache of being a historic property, many French colonial villas have found an economic niche by being restored and converted to restaurants. The refurbishing of the villa that is now Nam Phan Restaurant and the surrounding walled-gardens are as exquisite as the food.

TOP RIGHT Garden dining in the side yard of Nam Phan is a perfect place to look over the exquisite Indochine details of this period villa. The mix of Vietnamese styling with French colonial proportions define this Indochine architecture.

RIGHT Interiors of this private room at the Nam Phan restaurant have the luxurious calm of Vietnamese décor.

FAR RIGHT A small cloak-room has been converted to a humidity-controlled room for the wine and cigar collection.

LEFT AND FOLLOWING PAGES
A classic architectural example of the Style Moderne or Art Deco is the home of Mai Lam in central Ho Chi Minh City. The rich jewel-toned colors of Indochine Style are used in the sumptuous interior design of this historical home built in the 1930's.

Art Deco Villa in H.C.M.C.

Streamlined buildings with aerodynamic themes and rounded shapes were in vogue in 1930's French Indochina. The home of Mai Lam in central Ho Chi Minh City is a classic architectural example of the Style Moderne or Art Deco with Indochine adaptations. Mai has incorporated the rich jewel tones of Indochina—emerald, jade, garnet, and topaz mixed with torrid jungle colors of coral, chili pepper, mango, avocado, or bougainvillea fuchsia—in the exquisite interior design of her historical home built in the 1930's.

HaNoi remains the heart of VietNam, beginning in 1010 as the Imperial City for King Ly Thai To, to later become the capital of French Indochina in 1888 until 1945. HaNoi will celebrate its millenium anniversary as a capital city under the suzerainty of the Socialist Republic of VietNam.

France first established colonial headquarters in SaiGon but soon realized HaNoi was a market place for fine merchandise produced by skilled craftsmen in the surrounding countryside. Moving the political administration to this northern city recognized HaNoi as the cultural and economic center of Indochina. VietNam's economic growth has spiraled since becoming a self-ruled country with the capital city remaining a hub of art, industry, trade, and a population of experienced and educated people.

Aristocratic HaNoi is a mannerly and polished metropolis where there is a magnificence of archi-tecture that is readily apparent in the quality and quantity of buildings from the colonial era. The treasure trove of villas, mansions, and commercial buildings around the old French legation as well as those scattered around the abundant lakes and into the countryside are undergoing restoration. Study of these French Colonial structures reveals the layering of Asian components that constitutes Indochine architecture.

ABOVE **An entry door to a villa in HaNoi that is now an office. Elegant detailing blends French and Vietnamese aesthetics.**

OPPOSITE **While wood louvres are used in many countries, it is the Indochine world where shades of greens and blues are used with abandon. This bank in HaNoi glows in early evening light.**

RIGHT HaNoi's Opera House (Nha Hat Lon), built in 1911 was recently restored to its original grandeur. Vietnamese classical music is often presented in the 900-seat theater, so wonderfully decadent in original dark-mahogany woods and silk red-velvet interiors. The slightly decaying ambience adds to the historic atmosphere.

BOTTOM RIGHT One of the first examples of early Indochine architecture, this building designed by architect Ernest He'brard for the Ministry of Finance, now houses the Ministry of Foreign Affairs. It is certainly an architecturally mixed metaphor with its series of balconied-French-style doors shaded with tiled-eyebrow overhangs and pagoda-shaped roofs. Dressed in a pure pigment ochre color, this wonderfully fanciful building is situated at the apex of a grand roundabout that forms a radius to Dien Bien Phu Avenue in HaNoi, an avenue one might call Embassy Row.

LEFT Architectural streetscenes in HaNoi are a tangible museum of when the city was called 'the Paris of Asia'. The passing of time is evidenced in this grand old building; part of the architectural heritage from the French Colonial times. The balcony tile insets and jade-green shutters bring an Asian influence to an otherwise classic European design.

BELOW LEFT Here is a villa with a sense of French style in an urban dwelling, located in HaNoi. City properties are often entered from the sidewalk through a wrought-iron gate. From inside the home of Nathan Sage and Tranh Hoai Thanh, there is typically a double set of doors—wood louvre doors are for night-time privacy but allow ventilation while the wood doors with glass inserts are for cool nights—open to a small garden and a view to TuBac Lake.

Gardens of the Metropole Hotel are surrounded by wide porticos protecting their guests from sudden rain showers or tropical sun.

Hallways of the Metropole are once again as they were at the turn of the 20th century after a massive historic refurbishing of the hotel. Renovation design and planning was spearheaded by a husband and wife team, architect Nguyen Quoc Khanh and designer Le Quynh Kim Trinh; reportedly the most dynamic couple in all of VietNam and designers with exquisite taste.

A detail of the original iron brackets supporting wide overhangs on the porticos.

Sofitel Metropole HaNoi

Tamarind and plane trees shade the boulevards of HaNoi's former French Quarter: from Embassy Row to the Ministry of Finance roundabout, all around Hoan Kiem Lake and back through the commercial district to the historic HaNoi Opera House. There is a hotel near the Opera House that clearly evokes nostalgia for the Indochine Style— the Sofitel Metropole. Since first opening its doors in 1901 as The Grand Hotel Metropole Palace, the hotel has been at the centre of Indochina's social scene and counts as its guests, celebrities, and political figures from around the world.

OPPOSITE Sidewalks shaded by old trees, such as these around the Metropole Hotel, create the genteel mood of HaNoi.

LEFT The lounge just off the lobby has distinctive art deco style furnishings made locally in VietNam.

BOTTOM LEFT Staff in the Metropole Bar wear the traditional Vietnamese dress, the *ao dai*. They say the favorite drink ordered by foreign visitors is the 'house cocktail'—a potent mix of gin, dry vermouth, and a bit of cassis—called as you might suspect, the Graham Greene, after the writer who lived in the Metropole while writing *The Quiet American*. Other important guests staying at the Metropole through the years are the usual set of people traveling Southeast Asia in the early to mid-20th century; included in the list would be Noel Coward and Charlie Chaplin and then there was Jane Fonda who stayed during her visit in 1972 when she was protesting the American War in VietNam.

Villa La Résidence—HaNoi

At the end of a long lane, 500 meters or more from the main road, a gate opens to Villa La Résidence —a French colonial villa that is restored to perfection and with an art collection befitting of a museum. A mandarin ancestral hall-house joined to the original villa during the restoration project, successfully combines Vietnamese architecture with the colonial villa. The narrow public lane leading to this villa is wide enough only for pedestrians or *cyclos* (the ubiquitous pedi-cab/bicycle transportation found in VietNam), and all along the lane are gates that lead to traditional Vietnamese homes as well as old French villas.

On the day we were photographing Villa La Résidence, we parked at the start of the lane and transferred camera equipment onto a *cyclo*, piling the passenger seat so high with equipment that the *cyclo* driver had to lean sideways to see where he was going. As we trailed behind, the rest of the equipment balanced on our shoulders, we wondered why anyone would want to live where there is no convenient access. Only after spending time in this home did we understand: VietNam has always been a pedestrian society, and the daily walk home provides the time to stay in touch with the neighbors— learning the news of who got married, who had a baby, who is ill... The neighborhood becomes an extended family where good luck and misfortune are shared.

Loan de Leo, owner of the extraordinary Villa La Résidence resisted changing the walking path to a road as she wanted to keep the traditions of VietNam. When she first bought the villa, the area was known

OPPOSITE Vintage elegance of the façade of the Metropole Hotel is a fitting background for the Rolls Royce used in filming the 2002 version of *The Quiet American* starring actor Michael Caine.

LEFT AND BELOW Just inside the entry gate of Villa La Residence, a walkway allows views to the garden's lakeside landing. French inspired ornamentation is evident on the exterior of the villa.

as Nghi Tam Flower Village. Everyone in the village was engaged in flower farming and fields of blooming plants coloured the landscape. Those beautiful fields of flowers have disappeared with the encroachment of HaNoi's booming population into the surrounding countryside.

Loan de Leo is respected as a designer with vision as well as a knowledgeable and intrepid collector of fine objects. With a background in art history and archaeology acquired at the best universities in Paris, Florence, and Munich, she returned to Asia where she earned her PhD in Chinese studies and archaeology. She began collecting antique scrolls, Asian ceramics, and furniture traveling to Taipei, Kyoto, Hong Kong, and other Asian cities. Loan is a recognized researcher at the Institute of Archaeology of Ha Noi, where she specialises in Chinese and Vietnamese Ceramics. It is clear upon visiting Villa La Résidence that the accolades showered on Loan are understated. The home which she shares with her husband and two children is an extraordinary work of art.

Loan and her good friend—American architect Grover Dear of the architectural firm, ArchAsia (Hong Kong)—collaborated on the extensive renovation of the main villa and the integration of the mandarin ancestral hall-house. There is still an excitement in Loan's voice as she recounts the early planning of the home and how the design concepts were sorted out with the architect: "The decision to renovate the villa was the turning point that transformed my entire lifestyle while working in a new environment like HaNoi. Before moving back to HaNoi, I lived between Taipei

and Hong Kong, two very busy and dynamic big cities. When I returned to HaNoi, I fell under the spell of its charming little villages surrounded by bonsai gardens and flowers everywhere. It was a new experience to adapt to this slow pace of life where people have the time to chat over a tiny cup of green tea, then another and then another one—by the time the sun sets, you end up changing your mind about life downtown in HaNoi. Having said that, my first renovation was made on a townhouse in the middle of HaNoi and it took me four years and hundreds of visits to Nghi Tam Village to negotiate the acquisition of the villa. When at last, I had the villa, I called my good friend, architect Grover Dear, based in Hong Kong. Grover was so fantastic, he came over to see the house and he immediately felt the excitement that I felt.

"Because the house is right on the waterfront of a lake, there were new possibilities, new dimensions of entertainments where guests can arrive by boat and be welcomed into a lush tropical garden where scents of jasmines, gardenias, and lotus are floating in the air. We began to plan everything together—up to and including the details.

"At first it was not obvious how to turn a mandarin ancestral hall-house into a living space for a family with two young boys—my sons were in their early teens back in 1994. Grover did a wonderful job in translating all that was required to preserve the classic proportions of the house while giving our family a sense of spacious living areas, comfortable corners and lots of roofed terraces for a nice snooze in the afternoon or a lazy read on Sundays".

The main villa dates from 1910 and the ancestral hall-house dates from about 1889; both are classic in proportions and style. The renovation and expansion of the villa included removing walls to allow interplay of spaces. The challenge was in preserving the same column proportions and perspectives of the original salon for the new addition of a dining area and adjacent kitchen. In the main salon, an original and boldly designed fireplace-surround with a large mantelpiece displays some of Loan's collection of 15th century Vietnamese blue-and-white ceramic ware.

The timbered ancestral hall-house belonged to a high-ranking Vietnamese mandarin who served in the Imperial Court of Hue under the Emperor Thanh Thai of the Nguyen dynasty, and was probably a temple. In VietNam temples are used for study and contemplation or as meeting places while religious buildings are called pagodas. The hall-house was dismantled at its original site in Ha Tay province in northern VietNam and brought to Villa La Résidence to be re-assembled and incorporated with the existing villa.

The age of this type of ancestor hall can usually be determined by the date carved on the wooden centrepiece under the roof. The social standing of the mandarin is revealed through the quality of woodcarvings and the type of wood used: the fretwork and doors of this hall are executed in the exceptionally hard and enduring jackfruit wood while posts are made of Lim wood, a type of ebony. The doors open onto a verandah sitting area that overlooks the garden below. The mandarin ancestor hall-house is currently being used as an office, but will soon be converted to its

original function as a guest bedroom suite. The rosewood wall unit is a copy of a Chinese Ming dynasty collector's cabinet, and exhibits a fine collection of 10th to 16th century Vietnamese ceramic ware. The earthenware on top of the cabinet is early Han-Viet potteries from north VietNam. During the 2nd century BC through 2nd century AD there was a concentration of Chinese occupied territories in the north.

Vietnamese wooden panels, statuary and openwork carvings in the second floor hallway lead into the ancestral hall house. The red lacquered panels with carved characters on either side of the door are "parallel sentences"; traditionally hung on the two pillars of a family or temple altar. The text usually consists of a poem written by a scholar about the family or the full name and founding date of the temple. The Vietnamese characters are in the old Nom language, which uses Chinese characters but

BELOW Villa La Residence has many places to dine, each offering a different view and with a varied feeling. Informal lunch in this pergola surrounded by orchids and the beautifully designed stucco wall is enchanting.

BELOW A wrought-iron garden gate leads to the boat landing overlooking West Lake. A pathway made of terracotta pavers laid in losange shape are a reproduction of Tran dynasty, 15th century tiles used to pave floors of Imperial palaces.

OPPOSITE From the backyard, the waterfront entrance is through a covered verandah—a late afternoon teatime place to look at the garden and the lovely views toward other villages across West Lake.

Vietnamese intonation and semantics. The statues date from the 16th century and are part of a pagoda altar from a village in north VietNam. The floral wood carving above the doorway is lacquered *bois dore* (gold leaf on wood) and is made from jackfruit wood. Ornaments of this type are often found above ancestor altars.

The master bedroom was designed to be a quiet retreat in a busy household. As Loan describes: "The master bedroom and the ensuite bathroom are buffered from noise by overlooking the lake and the main staircase separates the rest of the house—so that we are completely shielded from noises, except the early morning bird songs. The bathroom is a piece of art in itself: it has an expansive view of the lake and is adorned by Frank Lloyd Wright-style latticed glass windows which incorporate the big flame tree into its space

OPPOSITE Just off the salon is a space dedicated to the observance of Buddhist rites. Antique carved wooden panels surround a fine old Buddha altar table. Bronze drums in front of the sofa are from the Dong Son culture dating from about 300 BC. Bronze object on center drum is an equivalent to a ceramic lime pot, 9th century. Tray on nearest drum has iridescent mother-of-pearl inlaid marquetry and a water pipe.

LEFT Pottery pieces on the salon mantelpiece are part of the de Leo 15th century collection of fine Vietnamese blue and white ware. Vase sitting on floor to the right of fireplace is a Han-Viet bronze jar from the Bronze Age. On the hearth are early pots used for the storage of lime which is one of the required ingredients for a relaxing quid of betel (a betel chew requires a *sirih* leaf wrapped about the betel nut with a sprinkle of lime powder). The large lamps are 19th century pottery from the south of VietNam.

OPPOSITE The villa renovation included opening walls between the columns. The open plan allowed an interplay of spaces when viewing the relationship of rooms. The difficult design task was to preserve the same proportions and perspectives of the original Salon into the new dining addition. This photograph looks toward the dining room and onward to the lakeside gardens.

LEFT Venetian-glass chandelier from Murano was found in old SaiGon when de Leo and her friend, Luc Lejeune were browsing for... "everything that smelled of old Indochine and I spotted the chandelier first, amidst Galle vases, Lalique glass, and Art Deco furniture". The chandelier is clearly a mouth blown Venetian glass from Murano with very delicate wrought iron work.

BOTTOM LEFT A lamp from the Han-Viet period. The jar has the recognizable 'green ash drop' technique, a special feature of that period. Exquisite hand-embroidered lampshade is from Asia Song.

RIGHT On the second floor is a hallway leading into the ancestral hall house. The wood panels, statuary, and open-work carvings are all Vietnamese. Red lacquered wood panels on either side of the door have carved characters and decorations with gold leaf applied. Vietnamese characters are in the old language Nom—a system created in the 15th century, borrowing the form of Chinese characters, but with Vietnamese intonation and semantic, to purposely irritate the Chinese by making the Vietnamese text difficult to cipher. Nom was very popular during the 19th century through the famous poems of Ho Xuan Huong. She was the first and only female poet that defied the Confucianist order of a male dominated society by writing the boldest erotic poems, however so subtle that her erotic innuendos had no match and remain unchallenged today.

and makes the morning shower a delight. Frank Lloyd Wright was himself inspired by Oriental latticework, and as the bathroom was a modern addition, I found it appropriate to revive Wright's translation of Asian proportions. To make the bathroom more extravagant, I asked an artist friend of mine to fresco the ceiling. He ended up spending two entire months on a ladder painting a Botticelli Venus on the ceiling".

The combined talents of Loan de Leo and archi-tect Grover Dear brought the diverse

architectural styles of VietNam and France together to become an integrated whole that honors details and retains individual expression. There is exceptional quality in all of the architectural components, in the textiles, the furnishings, and the collectible objects. Loan and her husband share their beautiful home with their two sons and two daughters. It is a home that represents a passionate love of living life to the fullest with the realization that surroundings are part and substance of the canvas of one's life.

LEFT When asked about this cozy room connected to the mandarin hall-house, Loan said: "The screen in this little alcove is a carved lacquer work of the 1940s in VietNam—very few pieces remain nowadays from this period. The scroll is a Chinese landscape style (19th century) I bought in Hang Zhou on an archaeological seminar in 1999. After this trip the hall-house was bought to recreate a mandarin house similar to those found in Su Zhou and Hang Zhou and of course to a smaller scale in north VietNam. A mandarin house would always exhibit several types of scrolls to show the high level of literacy of its owner.

RIGHT The timbered ancestral hall house (dating from about 1889) was dismantled at its original site in Ha Tay province in northern VietNam and brought to Villa La Résidence to be reassembled and incorporated with the existing villa. The exquisite fretwork and doors of this hall are executed in the exceptionally hard and enduring jackfruit wood while posts are made of Lim wood, a type of ebony. The doors open onto a verandah sitting area that overlooks the garden below. To accommodate a large project directed by de Leo, the mandarin ancestor hall-house is currently being used as her office but will be converted to its original function as a guest bedroom suite. The wall unit in the office is rosewood; a copy of a Chinese Ming dynasty collector's cabinet, custom made to exhibit a fine collection of 10th to 16th century Vietnamese ceramic ware. The earthen ware on top of the cabinet are early Han-Viet potteries from north VietNam where there was a concentration of Chinese occupied territories from the 2nd century BC through 2nd century AD.

ABOVE This original French colonial villa includes the most beautifully detailed period mantels and fireplace surrounds similar to this one in the master bedroom. The carved low table is the same design as the Vietnamese platform bed, however the small size indicates it was used as an altar table (see Chapter 5). Pottery on armoire are Han-Viet from Thanh Hoa coastal province where the Chinese colonies were concentrated during the first domination by the Chinese Han—the green ash drop technique on the beige glaze is considered to have preceded the green celadon glaze which was refined during the Ly dynasty in VietNam and Song dynasty in China.

OPPOSITE Placed at treetop level, a herald of angels blesses the master bathtub. Windows with an Indochine patterning of wood muntin can be folded open to create a completely out-of-doors feeling. The window designs are recognized as the work of Frank Lloyd Wright; however he actually borrowed this style of window muntins from Asian designs.

Villa of Simon Perkins

Simon Perkins, an Englishman now living in HaNoi, has worked in Asian countries for many years. He was delighted to find this old French villa when his company opened offices in VietNam. Perkins felt that the main villa was a good size to fit his needs and the second structure at the back of the property, previously used for staff, would make a perfect guest house. The buildings had been allowed to fall into disrepair; however the good bones and fine architectural elements were there. Perkins gives full credit for the inspiration behind the interior decoration and furnishings to his friend and interior designer Le Minh Hung: "We enjoyed the refurbishing", he said, "the restoration process was relatively painless for me, the Vietnamese are very skilled craftsmen, and I had the benefit of assistance from a very experienced letting agent, Julia Richards, who supervised the work if I was away on business. She loved to use my house as a reference for her other potential clients, and over the years has become a good friend and consultant, for any subsequent improvements." Renovating the villa and the guest house was a shared project but still demanded much dedication to bring the property back to its original look and feel—Perkins certainly provided the vision, time, and effort required to accomplish a fine renovation.

OPPOSITE The paved courtyard shared by the main villa and the guest house forms a private garden dining area.

LEFT A window with a view—from the kitchen, peering through tropical green palm fronds, there is a glimpse of the neighbor's house in a ripe papaya color contrasted with deep aqua awnings. The old wavy window glass panes soften the vision; as if in an old impressionistic painting.

ABOVE A large bathroom and tub is inviting with aquamarine walls... a divine backdrop for the white plumbing fixtures, the black and white tile floors and the organic touch of a natural bamboo storage unit.

DaLat: A French Hill Station

With a mandate of 'providing not only the services of a military camp, but also a complete administrative capital', the French Administration proceeded with building roads in extreme mountain terrain followed by the construction of a cog-railway to link the central highlands of DaLat to the coastal city of PhanRang. DaLat became so popular as a rest and vacation area, the Administration built a hunting lodge and luxury hotel; the Langbian Palace Hotel opened its doors in 1922 to accommodate tourists and enthusiastic hunters of wild-game.

An elaborate site plan for DaLat was drawn in 1923 by the Director of Service d'urbanisme, Ernest He'brard, architect and

OPPOSITE TOP Woodworking details of the pergola, balconies and rafter supports along with the roof ridge shape refer to an Asian influence in this 1930's French villa, now a museum open to the public. Hydrangeas are part of a long list of flowers and vegetables introduced from France.

OPPOSITE BOTTOM Cremaillere Railway Station in Le Petit Paris, DaLat, VietNam. A cog-railway began operations in 1917 linking this central highlands area from DaLat to the coastal city of PhanRang. It was a remarkable achievement considering the steep inclines to an elevation at DaLat about 1,500 meters above sea level.

LEFT A 1930's DaLat mansion, now a bit ramshackle, but still home to many families.

BOTTOM LEFT La Café de La Poste, the informal restaurant for DaLat Palace Hotel is housed in a charming French Colonial building.

ABOVE Cool mountain air, clear lakes, and evergreen forests beckoned the French out of SaiGon to the DaLat Hill Station. The DaLat Palace hotel has a commanding view overlooking the lake and town of DaLat.

urban planner for the colonial government. His utopian plan for a controlled resort for the elite was never completely carried out as it was considered 'too abstract' by the government in Indochina although praised in Paris. 'He'brard envisioned a perfect expression of his urbanistic principles: the separation of uses and races, made to seem organic by adaption to the natural terrain and building guidelines to control height, materials, density, and basic proportions' (*The Politics of Design in French Colonial*

Urbanism by Gwendolyn Wright). He'brard's grand plan sought to evoke a feeling of the French countryside with villas constructed resembling cottages in Alsace, Provence, Rhône-Alpes, and other provinces.

The DaLat skyline is a most unusual one with buildings ranging from provincial villas, Buddhist pagoda roofs, slender spires of Catholic Cathedrals to red-tiled Chinese temples... there is even a small replica of the Eiffel Tower in the middle of town built to ease the home-sickness of Parisians.

DaLat Palace Hotel

Since those early years the hunting lodge-luxury hotel changed ownership many times. During World War II, the lodge was forced to close when it was used as the accommodations of the Commandant of the Japanese Armed Forces in VietNam. After the war, the hotel was returned to the French Administration until 1958, when control of the hotel, renamed the DaLat Palace Hotel, was ceded to the South Vietnamese Government.

The hotel has a distinguished guest list that includes H.R.M. Prince Hendrik of Denmark, the Lord Mayor of London, and many heads of state, including the personal guests of Emperor Bao Dai.

General Manager of the DaLat Palace Hotel, Frenchman Antoine Sirot, is an avid historian of DaLat, known for his gracious hospitality, he generously gives time to recount stories of early years in DaLat: "During the early part of the 1900s, twenty percent of DaLat's population was foreign: more than 750 villas were built in the years during World War II, mostly by the French escaping war-torn Europe and wealthy Saigonese who could no longer sail back home for their holidays.

These villas are happily being restored but at the moment they are mostly crumbling. In 1991, a renovation of the Langbian Palace Hotel began along with an extension of the DaLat Palace Golf Club located across the lake from the Hotel. The original nine-hole golf course built by Emperor Bao Dai was extended to a championship 18-hole course; thanks to the exceptional climate there is Bent Grass on tee-boxes on all greens. The Langbian Palace

Hotel re-opened in May 1995 under the name Hotel Sofitel DaLat Palace. Renovations have retained the original colonial style of the hotel and have blended the old French style with a touch of traditional Vietnamese hospitality. The opulence in some of the restoration is breathtaking. Over 2,000 art pieces and sculptures adorn the rooms and public areas. Hotel Du Parc, our adjacent hotel reopened in 1997 under the name of Novotel DaLat after an extensive two-year renovation program. A unique feature of this hotel is the metal-caged see-through elevator synonymous with elevator designs in the 1930s. The splendour of a bygone era is evident in the finishing touches to both the hotels. Many of the rooms have private fireplaces."

BELOW LEFT The mezzanine balcony at the DaLat Palace Hotel offers a fine view of the mosaic floors of the lobby. Renovations restoring the hotel to its former splendor were directed by architect Nguyen Quoc Khan.

BELOW RIGHT French Colonial architecture with Vietnamese hospitality and service—the blending of these two cultures offers the best of both worlds.

RIGHT AND BELOW The French introduced flowers and vegetables from their homeland to DaLat. Emperor Bao Dai's summer palace flower beds are like European gardens in the selection of perennials and the beautifully designed maze of the parterre garden.

Bao Dai Palace—DaLat

Emperor Bao Dai had three palaces in Da Lat, all art deco designs of considerable style and detailing. The palaces were summer residences for the Emperor's family and to entertain French friends and foreign dignitaries. The palaces, designed by European and Vietnamese architects in pre—WWII times of 1933-38, were positioned with prominent views overlooking DaLat town and its mountain valley. During the French Protectorate, the Vietnamese emperors lost their power but remained symbolic of the royal family of Nguyen until 1945 when Bao Dai formally abdicated his position and was then exiled to France.

ABOVE One of the Emperor Bao Dai three palaces in DaLat, all art deco designs of considerable style and detailing.

The collection of Laotian-style Buddhist sculpture is outstanding at Haw Pha Kaew in Vientiane, the site of a former royal temple that was built in 1565 to house the Emerald Buddha. After a skirmish with Siam in 1779, the Emerald Buddha was stolen and has since been installed in Wat Phra Kaew in Bangkok. During the Siamese-Lao war of 1828, the Laotian Haw Pha Kaew was razed and then rebuilt in 1936.

Wat Si Saket was built in 1818 in an early Bangkok style, probably the oldest *sim* (sanctuary) standing in Vientiane. The *sim* is unusually situated... facing south, not east and is not parallel to the river. The row of columns form a verandah that surrounds the single-roomed sanctuary. The interior has as many as 2,000 niches with silver and ceramic Buddhas and the ceiling is decorated with relief mouldings that have highly carved pendants. The base of the pendants are in the shape of a lotus flower... a new element at the time in Lao religious art.

Phnom Phen—Cambodia

Cambodia's ancient history shines as a brilliant gem reflecting an artistic civilization in stark contrast to more recent times of cruel invasions, wars, and dictatorships that exiled or killed most of the population. Phnom Penh, the capital of Cambodia, was first known as Krong Chaktomuk, the 'City of Four Faces'. This name refers to the confluence of the Mekong, Bassac, and Tonle Sap rivers to form the site of the capital. Krong Chaktomu is an abbreviation of its lengthy ceremonial name given by King Ponhea Yat: Krong Chaktomuk Mongkol Sakal Kampuchea Thipadei Sereythor Inthabot Borei Roth Reach Seima Maha Nokor. King Ponhea Yat of the Khmer Empire, moved the capital from Angkor Thom to the site of Phnom Penh in 1434. This site fell to various invaders until 1866 when the capitol became the permanent seat of government under the reign of King Norodom I.

Soon to be called the Pearl of Asia, urbanized Phnom Penh was administrated by the French who engineered an expanded canal system to control the wetlands, built a railway and constructed roads as well as a port. Despite the brutal wars of the 20th century and destruction by the Khmer Rouge, the city retains some of its traditional Khmer architecture along with considerable colonial charm.

Recent political changes encourage cultural traditions and these values have promoted a new economy in tourism. Restoration of hotels and villas from the early 1900's and the construction of new hotels, restaurants, and residential buildings are revitalizing Phnom Penh and the nearby cultural sites.

Vientiane: The Walled City of Sandalwood

Quiet and leisurely Vientiane remains the capital of Laos, first designated with this status under the French protectorate in the late 19th century. The name Vientiane is a reminder of the French in its Romanized French version of ViengChang. The French colonial period is also remembered in a few faded villas and administrative buildings and the early morning smell of fresh French-style baguettes. There are many temples that are mainly Laos in character, however other historical influences are recognized as Siamese, Chinese, and Khmer.

BELOW AND RIGHT **Carol Cassidy** and her husband bought and refurbished this French colonial mansion in Vientiane to use as a weaving studio, workshop and showroom for Laos Textiles, the business they began in the early 1990s.

ABOVE French villas are seen as far north in Laos as Luang Prabang. This villa is now a restaurant serving traditional Laotian cuisine with gourmet presentation, i.e. *paa mok* (river fish steamed in banana leaf with an egg and coconut cream) along with *salat phak nom* (a specialty of Luang Prabang featuring a watercress available only in this area; it is a cress with a very delicate flavor).

Luang Prabang: A Historical Paradise

As the early morning temple gongs sound, the sacred atmosphere of Luang Prabang returns for another day. The daily enactment of spiritual life begins when young initiates parade in a single line, begging bowl in hand, through the narrow streets of Luang Prabang. Villagers offer a bit of rice, a symbolic nourishment to the young monks. With a long history of being the choice location for many temples (about 32 remain of the original 60) the unique landscape of Luang Prabang is shared with Royalty. A confluence of rivers is often the site of powerful energy which may well be the reason the First Lao Kingdoms, Lan Xang, chose Luang Prabang for the Royal Monarchy.

Luang Prabang province has a naturally beautiful setting amongst the mountains of northern Laos and the town of the same name is dramatically sited on the narrow peninsular (250 meters wide but less than 2 km long) that is formed by the NamKhan river joining up with the Mekong. This small town retains a quiet atmosphere of days long ago, in fact the population is not much greater than at the height of the French colonial era. UNESCO cited the town for the World Heritage List in 1995: "Luang Prabang is an outstanding example of the fusion of traditional architecture and Lao urban structures with those built by European colonial authorities in the 19th and 20th centuries."

A French Villa in Luang Prabang

Satri in Lao means lady and Satri Guest House just outside the main part of the town of Luang Prabang on Sisavangvong Road feels like a country home of a refined lady, where if you are fortunate, you have an invitation for a weekend. The villa is vintage 1905 built by the grandfather of Prince Souphanouvong (1909-95). The Prince lived in the villa from his birth until he was eleven years old. He was known as the Red Prince as he was an active nationalist and fought the French as a member of the pro-communist Pathet Lao. He served as President of Laos until he resigned in 1986.

It was in 1975 that the Communist Lao People's Democratic Republic took control of the small country of Laos, and it was that same year that the current owner of Satri Guest House, Lamphoune Voravongsa's parents sent her and her brother out of harm's way to live in Paris. Lamphoune grew up in France, living a comfortable life far different than those remaining in her homeland. Lamphoune longed to return to her country so as soon as the political turmoil eased she moved to the capital Vientiane where she started a business manufacturing and selling her own jewelry designs, and Laos silk weavings. She decided

BELOW The original living room is a comfortable salon for guests. Laotian artefacts are part of the salon's furnishings, to touch and to enjoy first-hand.

RIGHT Wood louvres of the door and window shutters reflect the quality materials used. A gallery extends the full length of the villa providing a shaded reception hall. The salon and bedrooms open onto the gallery where filtered light streams through along with the gentle cooling breeze.

BELOW An afternoon breeze lifts the silk draperies of a guest room doorway that opens onto the gallery hall. Rooms are tastefully furnished in period furniture from Laos. The Buddha statue is 17th century Lao.

to expand to Luang Prabang without any plans to own or operate a hotel until a villa became available that possessed such an extravagance of charm that it seemed there was no choice other than to buy the property. Realizing the possibilities of changing the villa to a boutique hotel, Satri House became a project suited to Lamphoune.

The renovation considered the historic nature of the property while adding comforts required by foreign guests. The footprint of the villa was re-organized to provide sitting rooms and large guest rooms with private bathrooms and the gardens and the grounds were beautifully set-to-order.

A unique feature of the villa is a long narrow gallery running the length of the house, somewhat like an enclosed verandah. The living room and bedrooms open on to this gallery that serves as a connecting hallway to rooms while providing a shaded buffer to the brilliant sun of Luang Prabang. The original living room is a pleasant salon with windows opening onto the gallery and to the gardens in the back. All of the rooms are large and airy with high ceilings to allow the heat of late afternoons to vent upward and out. Silk draperies and antique mossie (mosquito netting) nets over the beds are relics of luxurious times in the outpost of Luang Prabang.

Indochine Style's Alluring Imagery

Indochine Style is 'East-West fusion'—a design movement that grew out of French Indochina—to evolve as a tool used by twentieth century designers to add panache to timeworn classic solutions. Indochine Style's raison d'être, in fact its very foundation, rests upon the use of organic materials, authenticity, and subtle reminders of the Orient. The appeal of Indochine Style is ever apparent in fashion, furniture designs, textile motifs, cuisine, and architecture. The extensive allure of Indochine Style is recognizable in every design discipline.

PRECEDING PAGES, *(left)* Open rafters show the underside of roofing tiles, creating textural interest to the ceiling of the dining and kitchen pavilion. The carved doors are mounted on central pivots, allowing a full range of movement to capture every tropical breeze. The villa of Joelle Daumas and Kevin Snowball in Ho Chi Minh City. *(right)* A secluded garden with a built-in grill is a pleasant spot for informal dinners. An antique cauldron on a carved rose-wood stand serves as an ice-bucket. Nha Lien Hoa (The Lotus House) the home of To Hanh Trinh and Ray Mallon.

THE GLOBAL allure of Indochine Style encircles a far greater appeal than the mystique shrouding its geographic origins. 'East-West fusion', now a popular sobriquet, offers a design technique that freshens timeworn solutions. Twentieth century designers relied upon Southeast Asian concepts to imply a worldly and stylish character without overly ethnic reference. Indochine Style's raison dêtre, in fact its very foundation, included that which everyone wanted... organic materials, authenticity, and subtle reminders of the Orient. The addition of these elements easily meld into the décor of the grandest palace or modest abode, or completely comfortable in commercial or residential settings, provides panache to haute couture and infuses exotic taste to fine dining—with this versatility it is not surprising Indochine Style is put to frequent use.

Fashion designers revolutionized couture by replacing the corset with comfort and casual elegance: "It was in the name of Liberty that I proclaimed the fall of the corset....." cried Paul Poiret (1879–1944). By the 1920's, haute couture collections in the West borrowed lines of the *qipao* (cheongsam) and the *ao dai*, draping female torsos with glamorous sheath-gowns in the jeweled colors of Indochine. Silks from Asia appeared in saturated colors—topaz, coral, lapis lazuli, turquoise with Chinese button closures and mandarin collars—answering Coco Chanel's motto of 'nothing extravagant but everything luxurious'.

Furniture imports from Indochina made of natural bamboo and rattan appear in apartments from New York to Paris, pairing-down ostentatious decor while inserting a worldly-wise attitude. The adapted curvilinear shapes are visually softer and have an inviting scale; the same qualities to appear in mid-century Art Moderne salon furniture.

Textiles for drapery, upholstery, and a wide range of accessories appear in Western markets using the silks of Laos and Vietnam. Designs from the hill tribes of Laos and Cambodia are introduced in home furnishings for an ethnic look. Interior designers from around the world strive to create an Indochine ambiance in restaurants, including fusion menus featuring the cuisines of Indochina.

Architectural details with influence of Indochine are part of international themes for homes and commercial buildings beginning with the International Movement in Modern Architecture. Architect Frank Lloyd Wright's tour of the Far East culminated in his commission for a luxury hotel in Tokyo, The Imperial Hotel (construction 1915–1923). The dynamic concept of the hotel and his earlier Robie House in Chicago (1909) combined daring cantilevers, low horizontal lines, and steeply pitched roofs that indicate Southeast Asian design elements. Wood and stone craftsmanship of Wright's interiors feature parallel lines of the proportions easily recognized as Asian. Architectural academics agree with Wright's observation... "[my] work is considered the cornerstone of modern architecture".

Multi-disciplined designers found the elements of Indochine style act as an alloy, an ingredient that strengthens other components by adding a welcomed sophistication in a gentle and charming manner. Such is the extensive allure of Indochine Style that is recognizable in every design discipline.

LEFT Carved doors from Nepal and old stone sentinels welcome visitors to Nha Lien Hoa (The Lotus House).

ABOVE Door panels that the homeowners Trinh and Ray found in Kathmandu have been used in the garden, the master bathroom, and one of the guest rooms. The carvings depict Hindu symbols of fertility and scenes from daily life.

Homes
Nha Lien Hoa (The Lotus House)

Nha Lien Hoa near HaNoi is a contemporary home that stands as a prime example of the far-reaching appeal of Southeast Asian designs. In Vietnamese, Nha Lien Hoa means lotus house, a highly symbolic flower for the owners, Ms. To Hanh Trinh, a designer and co-owner of three outstanding restaurants in the HaNoi area and her husband Raymond Mallon, a writer and economist.

Trinh and Ray planned Nha Lien Hoa to maintain a cultural authenticity while meeting the requirements of their young family. Their design has accomplished a seamless blend of the old and the new; historical details and materials of old VietNam are neatly juxtaposed to current trends.

Being inveterate collectors of architectural materials, furniture, and art, Trinh and Ray started their concept of design upon locating two 19th century timbered ancestral hall structures. They decided to incorporate these architectural treasures into their new home along with other artifacts they found, including 15,000 bricks from the Han Dynasty (206 BC–AD 220) that were made in provinces along the northern border of VietNam. The timbered houses were transported to the building site along with the lot of bricks, and Trinh began to design the new home around these fabulous antiquities.

Trinh spoke of an ideal she abides by in her creative design process: "I read somewhere a quote which I like very much as it is so right for my principles while decorating our house as well as other places. It says 'Minimalism is a denial of—it costs nothing in

OPPOSITE The open and spacious verandah greets family and visitors to Nha Lien Hoa. Inset into the brick art wall is a relief showing a dancing Siva, flying warriors, and other details of Hindu worship. It resembles the sandstone sculptures of the Cham civilization, but Trinh prefers to think that the piece is a reproduction, rather than one taken from the site of the Cham Towers at MySon, Quang Nam.

ABOVE This lacquer statue of a *tien si* (scholar of the highest learning) receiving a warm welcome by his students upon his return to his village after being decorated by the Emperor, reflects the traditional respect reserved for learning in Vietnamese culture.

BOTTOM RIGHT These late 19th-century Ming Dynasty chairs in the salon have cushions with hand-embroidered designs of traditional motifs. The base of the lamp is a lacquered figurine of a Vietnamese servant, while the trunk was probably used by a rich or royal family from Hue. The large jar with dragon and cloud motifs is from Bat Trang.

OPPOSITE The formal salon at Nha Lien Hoa has a diverse collection of Southeast Asian objects that come together beautifully to complete this elegant room. A Chinese chair used in VietNam during the late 19th century sits beside an Art Deco sofa and chair from the colonial period. On the sideboard are lacquered statues carved from antique wood; antique ceramic vases from the Dong Nai province in south VietNam; and a tall Chinese celadon vase marked with 100 Chinese characters for 'Happiness'. Italian artist Valentina of La Casa in HaNoi created the ceramic and bronze sconce on the wall, while the large painting titled *Yin and Yang* is a lacquer and oil work by Bui Huu Hung.

taste or effort'. The idea equates to loneliness; you can't live in it; you can only occupy it". Trinh's fine sense of proportion and instinct for the textural interplay of materials, coupled with the valuable reclaimed objects, have resulted in a refined and gracious home with both comfort and historic value.

Stairs from the front entry lead to the open-air verandah that links the main house with the wing made up of the guest quarters upstairs and the formal salon downstairs.

The formal salon embodies the eclecticism of Indochine Style. Providing a handsome textured background for antique furniture and ceramics is the wall constructed from Han Dynasty bricks. The ageless appearance of these Han Dynasty bricks belies the fact that they are at least 2,000 years old. They are usually found in the Dong Trieu, Uong Bi, and Quang Ninh provinces (similar bricks are exhibited at the HaNoi and Ho Chi Minh City history museums. There is a wonderful variation in color, size, and texture, and some still have their glazing intact. The floor is a combination of handmade Vietnamese mosaic terracotta tiles and ironwood framing with bronze squares placed at crossings. The fusion continues with the furnishings and decor.

The guest quarter was constructed from an old house from Hai Hau district in Nam Dinh province. It is a typical ancestral hall-house and the quality of the large timber posts and clay tiles of the roof indicates that it belonged to a well-to-do family. No nails were used in the construction of traditional houses, as all joints were mortise and tenon, making it possible to disassemble and reassemble the structure elsewhere. The undersides of the roofing tiles are exposed and creates an attractive textured ceiling when seen through the rafters.

The master bedroom opens to natural light and gentle breezes from the canal flowing by the backyard. The bricks for the wall behind the bed were reclaimed from old pottery kilns in Bat Trang, while the red lacquered gold leaf panels on either side of the bed were originally doors of an antique cloth cabinet used by priests in Hai Hau, Nam Dinh Province. The polished floor is ironwood, which is amazingly hard and durable.

ABOVE The corridor provides a display space for a collection of objects from around Asia, including a brass jar from Nepal, a Vietnamese mother-of-pearl inlaid tiffin carrier and a bronze horse from China.

RIGHT A reading corner in the master bedroom opens onto a pergola garden. The draperies, embroidered cushions, and silk taffeta bedspread are from the Indochine-inspired collection of Asia Song Designs Ltd. by Valerie McKenzie.

OPPOSITE Trinh has a fine collection of textiles, including the gold-threaded Japanese *obi* hanging over the bed and the embroidered Vietnamese black silk blouse spread over the bed.

OPPOSITE The walls of the guest quarters bathroom are made of old bricks used to build kilns in Bat Trang. The sink is installed on antique stands.

LEFT A powder room in an unusual garden setting with loose river pebbles and a path made from slices of wood. The bamboo vanity is an old kitchen storage cabinet with a counter top made from Vietnamese slate with a natural cleft-finish.

ABOVE The customised red lacquered armoire in the guest bedroom was inspired by an antique Chinese cabinet and designed by their friend, Debbie Gauci. The vases, with an under glaze of blue and brown design and a crackled finish, are from Bat Trang.

RIGHT The vanity in the master bathroom at Nha Lien Hoa was custom designed by Trinh to accommodate a lavatory for herself and for her husband. She worked with a craftsman in a nearby village to execute the design. The tile mosaic backsplash was also designed by Trinh. Antique mirror frames above the vanity and the wood carvings on the lower shelf with crane and pine tree motif are all lacquered and gold-leaf finish.

OPPOSITE Chez Mark and Kim, an Art Deco chair and sofa sit happily with a French-styled lounge chair and ottoman in the living room. The old paintings were found in Ho Chi Minh City. In the mirror, we glimpse Mark and Kim as they tell us about their diverse collection of art objects.

Mark Acree and Kim Lion's Apartment

From spacious properties to the smallest of city apartments, Indochine Style provides sumptuous luxury without forfeiting cosyness. The Ho Chi Minh City apartment of American Mark Acree and Australian Kim Lion combines style and ease of living with much sophistication, where Art Deco sits happily alongside Victorian or colonial, or even a thoroughly modern style. This mélange of styles is supplemented by a fine collection of old and new paintings and objects displayed throughout the apartment.

LEFT Vietnamese silk draperies set a luxurious tone in the dining area of Mark Acree and Kim Lion's apartment. The marble-topped dining table came from an old house in Ho Chi Minh City—the Vietnamese base gives a decidedly Asian twist to the otherwise Victorian carvings. The bamboo chairs are new, while the polychromed wooden elephant on the table is a 15th century piece from Laos.

RIGHT Chartreuse silk-velvet was tufted to add texture to this sofa designed by Luc Lejeune's interior design company, NOOR. The reverse-painted 19th century panels behind the sofa depict the Four Eternals of Chinese mythology. The large wooden Buddha statue placed on the corner table is southern VietNam.

OPPOSITE A perfect blend of colonial and Vietnamese sensibilities is achieved by the mix of early 20th century Vietnamese rugs; a green vase from southern VietNam; polychromed wood statuary of the mythical unicorn lion, Ly Lin; and a rare leopard skin from the Central Highlands of VietNam, from a time when big game hunting was the sport of French colonialists.

Home of Luc Lejeune & Vu Dinh Hung

A very Indochine-styled loft in Ho Chi Minh City is the home of Luc Lejeune and Vu Dinh Hung. Luc is the co-owner of the Temple Club restaurant (featured on following pages). He moved from HaNoi to fast-paced Ho Chi Minh City, leaving the law profession to follow his passion for interior design and decoration. Luc's company, NOOR, is noteworthy in the design world of Southeast Asia, where it undertakes both residential and commercial projects. The flat is undeniably French due to Luc's heritage, but with overtones of VietNam, Hung's homeland.

Restaurants

Restaurants around the world are celebrating Indochine Style recreating an era replete with elegance and sumptuous comfort. The Temple Club in Ho Chi Minh City and the Ly Club in HaNoi are at the geographic center of the French colonial time and the interiors of each restaurant touch the heart of the era.

The Temple Club

In year 2000 the Temple Club owners, Luc Lejeune and Stella So, leased the second floor of an old villa in the heart of SaiGon, a house with fantastic architectural mouldings, vintage tiled floors, a high and undulating concrete ceiling, and a large porch overlooking the street. Lejeune's amazing sense of design and love of history is perfectly complemented by So's drive and business acumen.

As So relates in her effervescent manner, "It's like this: Luc and I are in a taxi heading to a meeting, he looks out the window at a pile of junk furniture, has the driver make an emergency, neck-braking stop, jumps out to pull a highly desirable picture frame or chair or some such object out of the heap, gleefully crowds back into the taxi with his treasure and off we go. I'm in the same taxi and never even saw that junk! I am busy in my head going over the details of the meeting."

OPPOSITE One of the main rooms of the Temple Club feels like a private salon, furnished with silk-velvet upholstered sofas and lounge chairs of the 1920s and 1940s. The brick walls of the original villa were restored but otherwise left untouched to give a natural look. The high, undulating concrete ceilings were painted white to provide an uplifting effect. The Art Nouveau rosewood screen could have been imported from France, but more than likely made in VietNam during the colonial time.

OPPOSITE Dames and Messieurs —restrooms in the Temple Club have reclaimed French doors with Vietnamese carvings on the solid wood and in the fretwork. The ebony wood surround is a decorative piece from a 19th century ancestral hall-house.

Their combined talents have made the Temple Club a restaurant offering the finest of Vietnamese food and a distinctive dining experience. Lejeune describes the sophisticated food they serve as 'Vietnamese home cooking', yet lunching at the Temple Club with a menu that includes steamed fish in a light sauce of lime and cilantro; grilled beef sausages wrapped in a lettuce leaf with basil and other herbs; a vegetable and tofu-curry dish and a salad of fresh young papaya strewn with mint, lime, and roasted duck, seems far removed from 'home cooking'. Sitting in the comfortable Art Deco lounge chairs, dishes are placed 'family style' within easy reach of everyone to dig in with chopsticks.

Terracotta floors and brick walls provide a warm, textured background for the elegant period interiors of the Temple Club. One of the main rooms of the Temple Club feels like a private salon, furnished in silk-velvet upholstered sofas and lounge chairs of the 1920s and the 1940s. The brick walls of the original villa were restored but otherwise left untouched to give a natural look. The high, undulating concrete ceilings are painted white to provide a fresh, uplifting effect to set off the brick walls and splendid furniture.

ABOVE A restroom with vintage appointments including old marble floors, a washbowl stand, and etched glass doors.

RIGHT A passageway is paved with restored vintage glazed tiles with the *fleur-de-lys* motif incorporated into a floral pattern using spare and uncomplicated lines.

OPPOSITE Yet more beautiful ceramic tiles pave the floors of the enclosed porch. The furnishings show the creative use of indigenous materials in Indochina.

RIGHT A custom-designed, silk lamp fixture lights the way for gentlemen.

FAR RIGHT The Ly Club lounge is dramatically lit by a series of silk lampshades, custom-designed by Ly Quynh Kim Trinh and fabricated by her company, RuNam Co. Ltd.

OPPOSITE In keeping with the owner's aim of supporting the performing arts of VietNam, the Ly Club offers intimate corners for artistic pursuits.

The Ly Club

Located in a classic building overlooking one of the city's many parks, the Ly Club is in a historic part of HaNoi with many architectural treasures; including the Opera House, the Metropole Hotel, and the stylish Government Guest House. The owners of the Ly Club say: "we have drawn inspiration for our business plan from the great dynasty of Emperor Ly Thai To who built the capital of his empire on the banks of the Red River in 1010. The Dragon Energy of these lands that are now known as HaNoi, gave scholars,

writers, artists, and performers an era of peace and creativity under the rule of the Ly dynasty. We wish to support the unique performing arts so that the traditions of VietNam may flourish".

The Ly Club offers an ambiance of ancient VietNam with a refined theatre setting on the first floor to showcase traditional music and drama. On the second floor, there is an elegant lounge serving afternoon tea and authentic specialties that are a mix of East and West, combining both worlds in perfect harmony.

ABOVE The villa has graceful
high, arched doorways, and
large windows. Here, a mirror
adds depth to the corridor.

RIGHT The enlarged versions
of these Art Deco style chairs
make them more comfortable
while maintaining the
graceful curves.

FOLLOWING PAGES The fashionable
Ly Club was designed by
architect Nguyen Quoc Khanh.
Indochine Style furniture
and furnishings create a
magnificent elegance in
the restaurant's lounge.

Indo-Chic Style: The Art of Living with Passion

I'm wearing a dress of real silk, but it's threadbare, almost transparent. It used to belong to my mother... It's a sleeveless dress with a very low neck. It's the sepia color real silk takes on with wear. It's a dress I remember. I think it suits me. I'm wearing a leather belt with it, perhaps a belt belonging to one of my brothers...This particular day I must be wearing the famous pair of gold lamé high heels. I can't see any others I could have been wearing, so I'm wearing them... Going to school in evening shoes decorated with diamante flowers...These high heels are the first in my life, they're beautiful, they've eclipsed all the shoes that went before.

—The Lover *by Marguerite Duras*

PREVIOUS PAGES (left) This pavilion—constructed using techniques from coastal regions and organic materials—is positioned to interact with nature. Here is an Indo-chic architecture that provides a serene atmosphere for rest and contemplation at the Ana Mandara Spa, Nha Trang. (right) Indo-chic restaurant Maxim's nam an opens onto the sidewalk with a lounge café that recreates the feel of 1920's SaiGon. See interior view looking out to the street in the picture at the beginning of this book.

ABOVE An Indo-chic lacquered container.

OPPOSITE The Indo-chic design of the lounge at the Moon River Resort near HaNoi plays with the rounded shapes of Art Deco—as seen in the wall display, shape of the bar and the oversized wicker lounge chairs—juxtaposed with the contemporary lines of the bar stools and the artwork on the back wall.

PASSION, perseverance, and style—these traits are part and parcel of the peoples of Indochina. Their cultural characteristics may be the result of surviving thousands of years of deprivation brought about by wars, invasions, conquests, and colonization. Against all odds, the peoples of these relatively small countries—Cambodians, Laotians, and Vietnamese—have persevered; they have passionately fought off the world's most powerful nations to gain sovereignty and to preserve their cultural heritage.

Philosophers, astrologists, and geomancy scho-lars have for centuries studied the subtle geological forces of Indochina. They write of a divine dragon energy, a magnetic force that runs through the Peninsular—the mountains of VietNam and Laos are the spine of the dragon's back, while Cambodia is the gathering basin, a watery place inhabited by dragons. It is said that an inexplicable force flourishes in the region, nourishing the people with steadfastness in purpose; with strength that can only be compared to a giant dragon. Architect Bui Khach Thanh, owner of HaAn Hotel in Hoi An, proclaims: "The energy in VietNam is very strong, an unknowable energy that seems to take over".

Be it *feng shui* and the geo-magnetic properties of the lands or the historical oppression that has shaped the cultures, an extraordinary force has empowered the Indochinese with an uncommon self-determination.

"Victoire appartient à persévérer.
(Victory belongs to the most persevering.)"
 —Napoleon Bonaparte

Victories won injected a renewed vitality — innate energy and passion are channeled into artistic creativity rather than toward the single, all absorbing activity of daily survival. Sovereignty has produced a certain *joie de vivre* born of peace; this newfound freedom has allowed an emergence of innovative ideas in business and the arts.

Southeast Asian designers industriously stepped forward into the global economy. They are injecting a certain cutting edge to the styles of Indochine by distilling basic elements into contemporary aesthetics. Indo-chic fashion and home furnishing products offer a fresh look, as in the simple yet distinctive container illustrated at left—here is a modernized shape, coated in traditional lacquer but tinted a smashing orange color.

A sub-trend to Indo-chic style is the shabby-chic movement in fashion and interior design. Shabby-chic is a fad inspired by genteel lifestyles gone threadbare, usually of colonial eras. Left behind, when the French withdrew from Indochina, were buildings, furnishings, and objects that aged with the passing of time. These remnants of a luxurious lifestyle fell into disrepair but were too valuable to discard. They represented quality heretofore unattainable by some, but to others a choice of style. There was also a segment of French expatriates who lived on the edge of the grand colonial lifestyle; they could not quite keep up and were forced to lead a 'shabby-chic' existence of worn elegance.

Jean-Jacques Annaud's 1992 movie *The Lover*, paints a vivid picture of a shabby-chic life lived by a French expatriate family trying to survive in the dwindling days of Française

TOP RIGHT Le Fenetre' Soleil
is a shabby chic tea room in
SaiGon, a comfortable place
to while-away the afternoon
drinking iced green tea or a
cool dragonfruit and pineapple
dessert. Old Art Deco chairs
and ottoman are in their
original fabrics.

BOTTOM RIGHT A girl with
attitude. She has made a chic
choice of colors: her traditional
ao dai is not white but hot pink,
and she is shaded by a melon-
colored paper parasol.

OPPOSITE A true Indochine mix
defines this chic design: an old
carved wood back-bar with
oriental motifs is combined
with luxurious gold finishes of
the bar front. Contrast these
bold statements of design with
the pure lines of modern stools.
There was no lack of passion in
designing this dynamic bar in
the Nham Phan restaurant
in SaiGon.

Indochine. In the opening scenes, teenaged Marguerite saunters leisurely to the rail of a ferry that will take her down the Mekong to a 'white' boarding school in SaiGon. The camera focuses on her high-heels; one toe placed on the edge of the freeboard reveals a worn but elegantly embroidered, gold lamé shoe that once must have danced in Paris salons. She wears an unlikely combination—a leather strap far too large for her slim figure belts her silk dress and her chapeau is a man's fedora. Marguerite's unconventional ensemble is threadbare yet stylish, it speaks to her individuality that is far different than that of the debutantes she will soon meet in school.

Thus shabby-chic has emerged as a design choice for those who desire understated refinement in a casual, comfortable manner. With an eye for elegance and classicism—be it architectural components, home furnishings or vintage fashion pieces—shabby chic is 'in'. The 'lived-in', worn-around-the-edges but classy look is achieved by recuperating old pieces and restoring old places.

There is a tidal wave of energy surging in Southeast Asia where designers from around the world are tapping into as a resource; into an atmosphere where they find an open and receptive market to experiment with original ideas. Since start-up costs to bring new products to market are relatively low in these developing countries; designers and investors are encouraged to freely design outside the norm, to try non-conforming ideas. French haute couture designer Pauline Trigere (1902–2002) encapsulates this new style with her motto: "Living, like dressing, should always be a result of passion, choice and chic".

Designers, hoteliers, and restaurateurs living and working in Southeast Asia have a legacy to draw upon, be it in architecture, craftsmanship, or fashion. At a time when the world is the consumer, Indo-chic, with its marrying of the old and new, modern and traditional, takes Indochine Style a step forward.

Designers and their Homes
Christina Yu—Ipa-Nima Vietnam Limited

"Les idées parfaites viennent de notre imagination magnifique," (Perfect ideas come from our splendid imagination) declares the flamboyant Christina Yu, designer of a slightly 'shabby-chic' line of high-end fashion handbags and accessories.

The Christina Yu brand, Ipa-Nima, ships from workrooms in HaNoi to top stores and boutiques such as London's Harrods or New York's Barneys. She believes that 'beauty has no borders', and her funky handbags and accessories are found in the wardrobes of the fashion-conscious everywhere. Yu hails from Hong Kong where she practiced law.

When her Australian husband was posted to HaNoi, Yu thought she would be leaving her glamorous life behind. Instead, it has flourished. "It is very much a story of fate and love. My husband moved to VietNam to set up the HaNoi branch of an international law firm where we both worked. I decided to move with him. A litigator is very jurisdictional; I had to give up my practice. So I abandoned myself to fashion, my true passion. I have always had a fashion vein in me and while I was working in Hong Kong, I moonlighted at a fashion magazine, so much so that I utilized all my annual leave for international fashion shows at my own expense."

OPPOSITE Deep purple, magenta, rice padi-green, and every shade of tropical color imaginable, combined with the seemingly impossible mix of silk, velour, feathers, leather, and bead work, bring glitz and chic to the Ipa-Nima collections.

LEFT An old Art Deco villa in HaNoi has been converted to an Ipa-Nima showroom.

RIGHT An alluring French poster from the 1920s has been updated to include a handbag and a feather boa designed by Christina Yu to advertise her brand of Indo-chic, Ipa Nima. OPPOSITE TOP The nautical lines of a steamship are clearly the inspiration behind the Art Deco home of Christina Yu and Mark Lockwood in HaNoi.

OPPOSITE BOTTOM The foyer of the Yu-Lockwood home resembles a work of art—the contrasting elements, the colours and the well-placed objects are nothing short of painterly.

In this northern city of VietNam, Yu found not only the freedom to explore her own creativity, but a workforce of talented craftspeople to help her execute her ideas. French influence has lingered among the peoples of Indochina to become an inherent part of their lives and their designs.

The chic world of Christina Yu and husband Mark Lockwood is not left behind at the design atelier. They live a busy, worldly life in their own Art Deco villa just outside of HaNoi.

LEFT The salon in the Yu-Lockwood home is filled with all the comforts of home—books, television (inside the armoire), and cozy upholstered furniture—Indo-chic style in a compact environment.

OPPOSITE A misty view of a distant village looks like a beautiful painting. The romantic master bedroom displays Christina Yu's knack of combining disparate objects into a distinctly unified whole.

LEFT The dining area is part of the salon, with the kitchen tucked into a portion of the room. Caprice seems to be the criteria for choosing objects, textiles, or furniture in the home, producing a riot of colors and styles.

ABOVE The salon is furnished with an assortment of vintage Art Deco chairs, a contemporary sofa, and a daybed. The silk-velvet embroidered draperies, cushions, and decorated velvet throw are all from Valerie's Asia Song Designs collections.

OPPOSITE The alfresco kitchen has cabinets made of natural stone and a wood-fired oven. The cat sitting above and to the right of the kitchen sink is not a porcelain statue but is the very lively family pet.

Valerie Gregori McKenzie—Asia Song Designs, Ltd.

Valerie Gregori McKenzie lives her life with passion, expressing a smart elegance in her work and personal life. She is a French designer with her own company, Asia Song Design Ltd. Her product lines include 'à la maison', a collection of furnishings and accessories for the home; a line of couture and resort wear; and her latest, 'YOGA', a line of exercise gear that combines chic and casual.

McKenzie lives in a very natural and stylish home, one that is filled with vivid colors and a relaxed atmosphere, surrounded by lush tropical gardens. The SaiGon River flows beside the house with rafts of water hyacinth gliding amongst tandem barges—work and pleasure river craft sharing the same space with the vibrant blue flowers. She says, "I design products for my label that offer customers an opportunity to experience having a piece of paradise no matter where they are in the world."

The Asia Song brand of home furnishings and effortlessly chic designer clothing carries the stamp of the designer's personality. McKenzie designs according to her personal tastes and colorful lifestyle. Her designs are a fusion of European classical elegance and delicate Asian craftsmanship—an Indochine Style with a slightly 'shabby-chic' edge.

OPPOSITE The hallway from the dining room looks across the breezeway toward the dressing area of the bath pavilion. The large, dark aqua jardinière is from VietNam.

TOP LEFT A tangle of ginger, papaya, elephant ear, and coconut trees surround the bathroom pavilion. The house was too small for the bath suite McKenzie wanted so she built an outdoor bathroom pavilion in the garden. Restored shutters are the only window coverings, the walls are made of wood and stone, and the thatch roof is similar to those that are used in rural areas.

BOTTOM LEFT Tara McKenzie's fanciful bedroom has a balcony with a view of the expansive river. A curtain of hearts made by Tara, sections her bedroom from the bath.

Indo-chic Dwellings

Yves-Victor Liccioni is the deputy director of the Ipa-Nima line by Christina Yu. Liccioni travels the world but home is his *l'appartement* retro-chic in central HaNoi, overlooking the beautiful Hoan Kiem Lake. An oversized upholstered chair is an invitation to relax in his salon in this French era building. The cochenille-red silk shade of the vintage floor lamp reverberates the color themes established in old Indochine prints and accessories in an otherwise monochromatic interior in tones of bright white and dark woods. Details of the fireplace surround are period Art Deco that appeared in 1930's Vietnam. Liccioni has stylishly adopted elements from the past into a modern setting to express his own individuality.

Home for American Daniel Leavitt, who works with the United States Agency for International Development (USAID) as Health and Humanitarian Program Manager, is a study in modernist-chic. The flat has smart, clean lines highlighted by natural light sweeping in from a large skylight. The ceilings and upper edges of the walls covered in lengths of bamboo, add an organic touch to an otherwise modern setting. Leavitt's black-and-white painting, sleek sofa design and khaki walls are a bold statement balanced by the red splash of an area rug. A tall white canvas awaits Leavitt's inspiration but in the meantime provides a stark and handsome element to this room.

OPPOSITE An oversized chair is an invitation to relax in Liccioni's salon. The red silk shade of the vintage floor lamp reverberates the color theme for accessories in an otherwise monochromatic interior.

ABOVE The view from the kitchen window of Leavitt's flat looks upon a bit of history in HaNoi. Just outside the window can be seen a colonial balcony of the apartment next door that shares a back-courtyard with television antennae, an early Vietnamese building and a view of an aged copper dome of a grand French colonial building.

NEXT PAGE French doors in the Indo-chic apartment of Daniel Leavitt lead to a rooftop garden.

RIGHT Silk lanterns and embroidered draperies are part of the décor that create an Indochine style interior at Vine Wine Boutique Café and Bar .

OPPOSITE The ceiling treatment of draped silk produces a softly billowing movement and a warm luminosity in one of the dining rooms.

Restaurants

Creativity is the operative word in restaurants, Indo-chic concepts in the decor complement the imaginative menus of these restaurants. Master chefs are rearranging the ingredients and cooking methods of traditional Indochine cuisine to create gourmet taste sensations heightened by the dynamic atmospheres that remember the best of Indochina while embarking on new concepts.

Vine Wine Boutique Bar & Café

The atmosphere of Indo-chic created in the dining rooms and lounge are a fitting backdrop for the passionate work of restaurateur Donald Berger. Berger is the managing partner for the Vine Group's Boutique Bar & Café in HaNoi. He is Canadian, has circled the globe as an executive chef for the best restaurants, and spent time studying winemaking in the vineyards of Burgundy. Berger lives by the quote: "life is too short to drink bad wine". The Vine Wine Boutique Bar & Café received an Award of Excellence by the prestigious Wine Spectator Magazine for having one of the best wine lists in the world. Excellence in food, wine and enjoyable décor have assured this café a favoured local pub in HaNoi.

ABOVE Red, gold, and purple set a chic Asian tone for the dining room and lounge of Apsara Inn. The lacquered floor urns are from Burma and the large triptych is by Haude LeBars, a French woman living and painting in Vientiane.

Aspara Inn

In 1909, a French woman, Marthe Bassene, wife of a colonial doctor stationed in Luang Prabang, wrote in her private journal: "Oh! What a delightful paradise of idleness this country protects, by the fierce barrier of the stream, against progress and ambitions for which it has no need! Will Luang Prabang be, in our century of exact sciences, of quick profits, of victory by money, the refuge of the last dreamers, the last loved ones, the last troubadours?"

Luang Prabang has changed little since French colonial times; it has remained a quiet and small town with less than 20,000 residents. The town stretches along a peninsular where the northern Mekong meets the Nam Khan River. It is a place so steeped in history that Unesco's World Heritage program is currently engaged in classifying some 700 buildings for conservation.

Ivan Sholte visited northern Laos at a time when he was weary of running a hotel in Thailand and living in bustling cities. His longtime dream was to own and operate his own small hotel. Sholte was on the search for a property that he could transform into an inn with a modern Asian theme. Visiting

Luang Prabang, he came upon a small inn for sale where the Nam Khan River runs parallel to the town road, Thanon Kingkitsarath. The site was perfectly located, being a short walk from the center of town, and Sholte saw the possibilities a renovation could bring about, especially the exciting prospect of operating a restaurant serving his own creations. Sholte's dreams are realized in the Apsara Inn's menu that includes a perfectly grilled Panin river fish with lemon grass and tamarind sauce, an exquisite array of soups and desserts, such as Nashi pear poached in a ginger/lime sauce with homemade coconut ice cream. Seen as

a work-in-progress, Sholte is well aware that the realization of a dream is the beginning of an on-going affair.

Meanwhile, Ivan Sholte's inn provides solace for weary travelers with its large and airy rooms with a view of the river. There is restful ambiance in each room with their polished dark wood floors and white walls; where multiple teak louvred windows can be closed to shut out the world or opened to let in the river breeze, where silk curtains billow in the breeze and exquisite bed linen spell comfort. The outdoor balconies are ideal for watching the quiet world of Luang Prabang saunter by.

ABOVE The high ceilings and large windows with carved wooden transoms in guest rooms at the Aspara Inn lend to the breezy and restful ambiance.

OPPOSITE The owners of Wild Rice Restaurant had wanted to 'open' the dining room with windows, but sadly their villa was within a few feet of the property next door. They struck upon the innovative idea of installing a glass wall and planting bamboo in the space between the two buildings.

Wild Rice Restaurant

Wild Rice Restaurant is located in a classic French villa in HaNoi. While some attributes of the colonial architectural period are left intact, the vibrant interior design is chic and innovative with the spare, clean lines offset by edgy modern art. The service is gracious and friendly in keeping with the best of Vietnamese traditions, a true complement to the fine food and creative décor. There are subtle blends of influence from traditional homey foods to imperial cuisine, from East Asian cuisine to French food. Exhibiting Vietnamese fine art is a priority of the owners of Wild Rice—Pham Ba Khanh Thinh, To Hanh Trinh (whose home, Nha Lien Hoa, is featured in a previous chapter) and Tran Vu Hoai.

Maxim's nam an

Exemplifying Indo-chic at the top of the universal cachet is Maxim's. This restaurant is on the posh side of elegant dining in Ho Chi Minh City's District One—SaiGon. Located next to, and at one time even part of, the historic Majestic Hotel on Dong Khoi Street (the former Rue Catinet). Architect Nguyen Quoc Khanh and designer Ly Quynh Kim Trinh are also the owners. Their combined talents restored this old building that has undergone many incarnations as a theater to become the new Maxim's. They incorporated the theater elements of the building into their design. Indeed, upon entering the main dining room, the bar literally takes centerstage. Maxim's in Ho Chi Minh City has reached beyond the décor de belle époque of the original Maxime à Paris to achieve a sumptuous Indo-chic atmosphere.

RIGHT The balcony of the old theater is now part of the dining area at Maxim's nam an, with a view of the bar and diners below. Walls of the deepest wine tones set a tasteful background for art. The luminaire lamps with silk shades are designed by Ly Quynh Kim Trinh.

OPPOSITE A fashionable bar takes centerstage in the lower dining salon. The silk tufted wall panels and stage stairs to the upper balcony are reminders of the restaurant's theatrical origins. The stage floor has an abstract design executed in ebony and set into the parquet floor.

LEFT Dining alcoves with carved wooden frameworks resembling large opium bed frames, provide intimate spaces within the restaurant. Strikingly large, hand-painted lotus blossoms are a recurring theme throughout the restaurant.

Indo-Chinoise:
The Artistry of Indochina

Youngest daughter of the Black River
With the sweet, fanciful name of Vu Chua Pua,
Nimbly stitching and embroidering,
Ninety-nine silk pouches already completed,
A gift to her loved one of the Red River.
He carries them on his way to bargain for buffalo.
Youngest daughter of the Black River,

With the sweet, fanciful name of Vu Chua Pua,
Nimbly sewing trousers of silk,
A gift to her loved one.
He carries them on his way to bargain for pork....
   —Song of the Daughter-in-Law,
    H'mong Ethnic Group
    As recounted in Neos Guide-VietNam

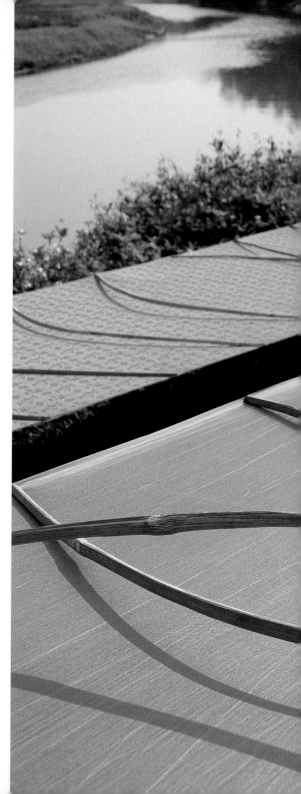

THE ARTISTRY of Indochina flows like a river of silk of varicolored strands woven into a tangible whole, into a fabric of magnificent richness. Indo-china is the loom, China and India provide the warp and the weft. The weavers are the people of Indochina and their product is Indochine Style.

Endowed with a creative nature, the Indochinese applied ingenuity in utilizing available raw materials from their bountiful environment. Archaeological excavations of the Dong Son civilization in Northern VietNam reveal a sophisticated society that utilized bronze and iron from as early as 1,000 B.C. Large stone drum-shaped objects uncovered in Northern Laos bear engravings similar to those seen on the bronze drums of the Dong Son. The Plain of Jars sites in Laos contain hundreds of enormous containers made of composite materials or carved stone; some weigh as much as 600 kg to one ton each. The jars are thought to be sarcophagus or perhaps used for wine fermentation or grain storage.

Indochina's population, consisting of many ethnic groups, have applied their artistic talents in the adaptation of foreign influences since ancient times. Life's basic requirements presented opportunities for aesthetic interpretation and invention; finding expression in their textiles, basketry, pottery, ceramic arts, copper, and lacquer wares. Their ethos is articulated in the fabrication of clothing, musical instruments, tools, toys, housing, and furniture. Thus, Indo-Chinoise designs boast a delicate lightness with unassuming sensuality that was handed down from generation to generation—objects that are remarkable for their beauty, practicality, and com-mercial value constitute a precious cultural legacy.

PREVIOUS PAGES *(left)* **A papaya-colored wall is a splendid background for the Vietnamese bamboo bench, silk pillows, and framed photograph of a young girl sitting on a bamboo platform table.** *(right) Gai thuong*, **a minority girl from the Highlands, water-color on silk painting by artist Mai Long.**

ABOVE **Glaze designs are hand painted in the pottery village of San do Hi Bat Trang, VietNam. After firing, the gray designs will fuse to the clay base changing to a glossy, semitransparent glaze in subtle hues of blue and green.**

OPPOSITE **Silk fabric is stretched to dry—after having been woven and dyed by hand—creating a seemingly endless river of silk.**

Bronze Drums

Archeologists have identified an early Bronze Age culture (circa 1,000–1 BC) in far northern VietNam, near China, where metal artefacts are found that were made using the lost-wax metal casting technique. This method of casting involved utilising a wax mould in which molten metal is poured. This period is named Dong Song culture and is notable for its elaborate bronze kettledrums. These kettledrums, some as large as 65 cm in height, have intricately incised patterns and pictographs revealing extraordinary details of daily life. Being idiophones—instruments made of a resonant material like wood or metal that make a sound when struck—they required no other implement or membrane to produce a sound. Bronze kettledrums of this type have been found throughout Indochina and Indonesia.

RIGHT A teak-wood platform table is used as a writing desk by a calligrapher in HaNoi. The wood carving on the apron is a fine example of Vietnamese designs using subjects of nature in uncomplicated, fluid lines. The Art Nouveau movement began late 19th century; this table is early Vietnamese of about the same period.

OPPOSITE An old house in HaNoi has antique Vietnamese furniture that incorporates the rococo shell motifs of 19th century Europe. Note the mother-of-pearl shell marquetry that is a specialty of VietNam craftsmen.

Furniture

Platform beds are a furniture form that is broadly used as coffee tables in Indochine interiors throughout the world; its genesis is China where the *kang* platforms were large and often provided a charcoal stove for heat. Indochina adapted the form, particularly in VietNam, where the platform bed is designed to be only 35 to 40 cm off the floor to provide a comfortable seating height and is placed in the main room of a traditional house. Guests, particularly the older ones, are invited to sit down for a cup of tea, to chat and chew betel nut. Indeed, there is a saying in Vietnamese *Mieng trau mo dau cau chuyen* (literally start the conversation with a chew of betel nut). At night, the wooden platform is converted for sleeping by spreading a woven mat of split bamboo, straw, or fine reeds to serve as a mattress. Wealthier families may have platform beds made from fine woods such as ebony or rosewood with deeply carved aprons, and these are sometimes lacquered with a gold leaf finish. Smaller platforms are used in temples and pagodas as altars to place elaborate offerings during special occasions such as the death anniversary of an ancestor or the veneration of gods or for Tet (the Lunar New Year celebration). Indochine adaptations of platform beds often appear in lighter woods such as teak and have limited amounts of carving.

Art Deco and the Style Moderne (appeared at practically the same time) became popular trends in reaction to the complicated floral patterns, sinuous lines, and free-flowing curves of Art Nouveau. The Paris Expos of 1924-25 along with the discovery of Pharaoh Tutankhamen's tomb in 1922, set into motion the new and fashionable style of geometric patterns. The stepped forms of Art Deco seen in corbel-arches and chevron decorations are considered Egyptian pyramidal motifs. Eager to continue a stylish mode, the French Empire in Indochina eagerly incorporated Moderne elements in architecture and furniture. Streamlined buildings with aerodynamic themes and playful decoration were in vogue in SaiGon and HaNoi.

RIGHT The light refraction qualities of mother-of-pearl can create a totally different range of colors depending on the angle of viewing or the light source. A variety of shellfish in the waters of the South China Sea is the source of this beautiful iridiscent material used as inlay. The shell is cut into sheets and polished before cutting the delicate floral designs, butterflies, birds, people, and other winsome symbols. This image is a detail of a serving tray in LIM Du Minh's collection.

RIGHT The flowing lines of this Art Deco chair are interrupted by the horizontal intersection of the planes of the arm rest. There is a suggestion of an Oriental influence in the arm rest. Photographed at the shop, Nguyen Frères, owned by Nguyen Thi Tu Anh.

OPPOSITE This remarkable late 18th century Vietnamese chest is an exquiste example of fine cabinetry and mother-of-pearl marquetry. This chest was made in VietNam, re-discovered by LIM Du Minh in France and brought back to VietNam for restoration and repair. According to Minh: "Inlaid mother-of-pearl of this quality can only be repaired properly by Vietnamese artists. In VietNam, the workmanship and colours of mother-of-pearl are more delicate." The blue-and-white porcelain ware was recovered from the Vung Tau Cargo, which was salvaged from the wreck that went down in the South China Sea in 1692, enroute to Europe.

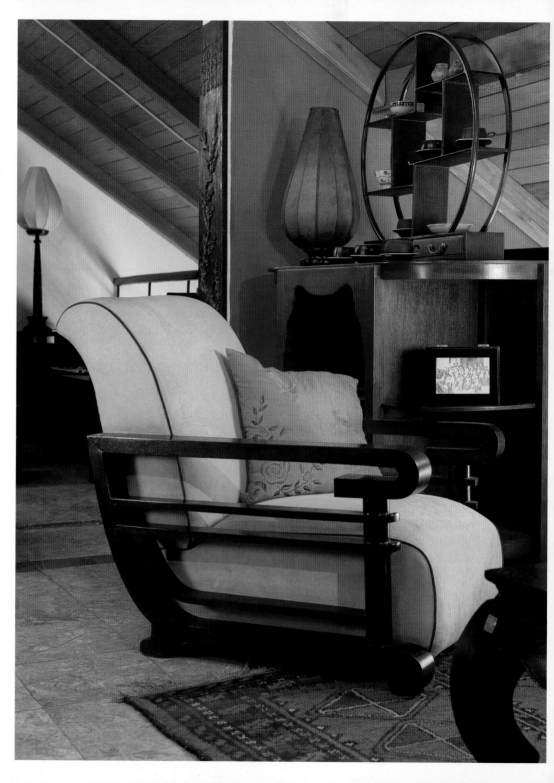

Silk

An early morning sound in a silk-producing village is the rhythmic, wooden clickity-clack of shuttles being thrown by weavers at their hand-operated looms. Walking the narrow lanes in such villages, the complete silk making process may be seen: there are some residents engaged in growing mulberry trees for the leaves to feed silkworms, others are spinning thread from the cocoons of the silkworm while some are dyeing the thread or weaving or operating shops selling fabric. Silk is as common in Indochina as cotton and linen is in the West; clothing made from silk is everyday wear in these parts. The silk trade was inherited from neighboring China during the times of Chinese occupation, but it has given rise to a variety of weaving and dyeing techniques specific to each region of Indochina.

RIGHT Patterns for different designs are determined by the sequence and shape of holes in these cards. In most silk-producing villages in Indochina, card pattern machines have not been upgraded to computer-generated patterns.

BELOW RIGHT Weaving is primarily the work of women. The fine white powdery dust on the floor is the by-product—silky lint.

OPPOSITE Natural and synthetic dyes are used in the small, cottage-industry of silk production. Men are actively engaged in the dyeing process.

OPPOSITE Peering into the backyard of homes in the silk-producing village of Lua Ha Dong near HaNoi, one sees a colorful sight of newly-dyed silk drying under the sun.

LEFT Shops display silk in an irresistible array of texture, pattern and color. Touching is definitely allowed, even encouraged, in silk shops. Vietnamese silk is fine in texture and has a soft-hand.

FOLLOWING PAGES Silk lanterns, created by Ly Quynh Kim Trinh for her company Ru Nam Co. Ltd., come in multiple shapes and colors, and enhance the decor of the Ly Club in HaNoi. The applied decorations are embroidered by hand.

Weaving Techniques in Laos

Weaving in Laos is an art form, a cultural tradition that is part of a family's heritage. Grandmothers bestow a legacy of favorite weaving patterns upon their daughters and granddaughters. Indeed, some patterns are quite rare with only a few families holding onto the knowledge of how to weave them. The value of a woven cloth depends on the complexity of a pattern: the number of rows that make up a pattern, the number of colours used and the number of threads in the warp.

In weaving terms, the warp consists of threads running from the weaver lengthwise; the weft threads cross warp threads by way of a shuttle that moves from right to left then right again, resulting in woven cloth. Weavers in Laos use different styles including tapestry, whereby the weaver makes a plain-weave pattern using multiple colors, creating a somewhat abstract effect. The pattern is the same viewed from the front or the back. Supplementary weft weaving is the name given to a textile that has the appearance of an embroidered cloth; it is in fact completely woven using supplementary weft threads of different colors to make additional patterns on the base cloth. Again, the pattern remains the same viewed from the front or the back. *Ikat* is yet another style of weaving found in Laos as well as in Indonesia, Japan and India, where a pattern is determined by bundling yarn then dipping the bundles into dye, a technique known as resist-dye. The pre-dyed yarns are then woven, resulting in the pre-determined pattern. *Ikat* cloth patterns have a muted motif, as colors appear to bleed one to the other.

Lao Textiles—Carol Cassidy

Upon arriving in Laos in 1989, American weaver Carol Cassidy found a weaver's paradise—a country with a rich history of weaving and a large repertoire of design motifs. She first came to Laos as a textile expert with the United Nations Development Program and then stayed on to work with local women, teaching them how to meet current market demands for woven cloth. Cassidy started a weaving studio and a new business in Vientiane named Lao Textiles. Cassidy also redesigned the looms used in Laos to produce wider fabrics and longer lengths, targeted at the international home furnishings industry. The traditional looms in Laos limited the length of cloth that could be woven to no longer than a skirt-length or a shawl-length. The new hybrid loom maintained the 'vertical heddle' design mechanism that is unique to Laos. By changing the width of the loom and adding a back roller beam, longer warp threads could be used and an even tension maintained when weaving wider and longer fabrics and while weaving the complex designs.

Since 1993, Cassidy has worked with farmers in various parts of Laos to raise local mulberry and provide Lao Textiles with varieties of wild silk. Although the quantity of silk produced has increased—up to 400 farmers in the Xiang Khouang and Luang Namtha provinces have been involved—the supply is still insufficient to meet demand, and Cassidy has had to buy additional silk for the warp threads from China and VietNam. Cassidy has trained her staff in color theory and dye techniques. All of the dyeing is done on site at the studio in Vientiane using dyes of the highest quality available in the industry. Cassidy remains enthusiastic after years of work in Laos: "We are weaving with passion, creating art. The Lao Textiles team produces high quality silk textiles that combine an ancient craft with a modern eye. Our focus is quality and creativity, using the weaving traditions of Laos and bringing them into the future. We have had the same team for the past 15 years, we all enjoy our work and working together."

RIGHT School girls in Luang Prabang wear their uniforms, a traditional Laotian *sarong* (worn as a long skirt) called *sin*.

OPPOSITE Carol Cassidy in a workshop at her Vientiane studios of Lao Textiles.

RIGHT Woven products of
Lao Textiles are to be found
in galleries and museums
throughout the world.

BELOW RIGHT The showroom of
Lao Textiles is on the first floor
of the French colonial villa.
Their exquisitely crafted wall
hangings often take months
to complete; for the most
complex designs, only two
centimeters are woven per day.

OPPOSITE More than 40 weavers,
mostly women, are employed
at Lao Textiles. Here, Mrs.
OnKham holds the reed in
her left hand and the wooden
shuttle with the weft thread
in her right. She is weaving an
ikat fabric designed by Carol
Cassidy called *Dok Champa* or
frangipani, the national flower
of Laos.

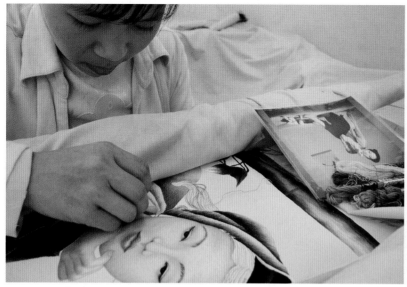

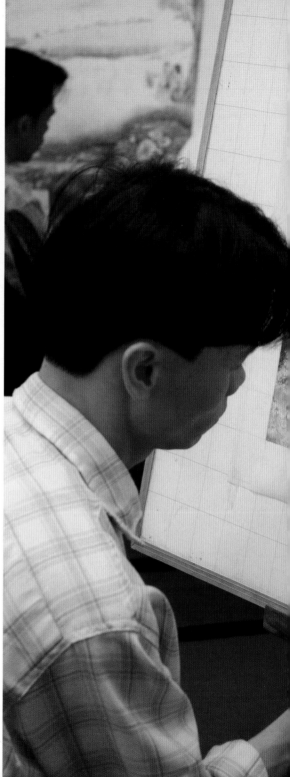

Art

Artists from Indochina have penetrated the global fine arts market with stunning images of the lands and people they know; techniques relate to French Impressionists paintings from the late 1800's, begging the question if French artists first saw paintings from French Indochina that influenced their art works.

Close study of French Impressionist Henri Matisse, Camille Pissarro, or Mary Cassatt shows Asian influence just as Paul Gauguin's work was influenced by the South Seas.

The paintings of Vietnamese artist Mai Anh depicting the rituals and daily life of contemporary Vietnamese women, has a dream-like quality and is a reflection of deeply-felt emotions. Her painting titled *Basket of Salt* is her interpretation of the mystique of the market women at Diem Pho. She tells of her early years in Ngan Pho

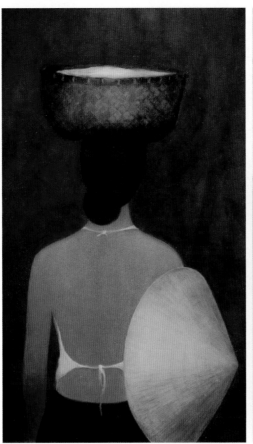

RIGHT *Basket of Salt—Diem Pho Woman* by artist Mai An shows a woman setting off to the market to sell a basket of salt. The white halter top of the woman from Ngan Pho is a *yem*, the traditional bra used by Vietnamese women made from cotton or silk. Married women with children may work around their homes in the *yem* but when going out they cover-up with an outer garment such as the very feminine *ao dai*.

FAR RIGHT Artist Mai Anh at work in her studio.

OPPOSITE The Apricot Gallery occupies a classic French villa in HaNoi's Old Quarter. The inner courtyard of the villa linking the galleries is a tranquil garden of tall bamboo and fish ponds.

village in Hau Loc district of the Thanh Hoa province, where women are known for their beauty: "This painting is a precious memory of times spent with my father (he was a writer) speaking of the beautiful women of the province—the beauty of their translucent skin and fair complexions." Mai Anh paints from heartfelt experiences, and explains her work as: "a reflection of my interior garden, a constantly flowering garden of emotions". Each of Mai Anh's paintings is original—she makes no duplicates and does not prepare beforehand what to paint. She allows the moment and the canvas to speak to her. Mai Anh was so attached to the *Basket of Salt* painting that she deliberated for a long time before deciding to sell the painting to an English woman. Mai Anh's husband, Le Trung Thanh, operates the Ngan Pho Gallery in HaNoi's Old Quarter, which represents not only Mai Anh's work but also that of other artists from VietNam.

Embroidery

Embroidery as an art form was adopted from the Chinese; however Vietnamese embroidery has distinguished itself by its craftsmanship and extraordinary clarity of color. Embroiderers from the city of Hue are particularly acclaimed for the artistic quality of their work, noted for its dainty designs and subtlety. Embroidery as art for aristocratic families was founded by Tran Quoc Khai in the 17th century. The mother of Emperor Bao Dai of the Nguyen dynasty (1925–1940), Lady Hoang Thi Cuc, was an expert in embroidery. She considered the craft to be a combination of Asian and European artistry and some of her work is on display in France as well as VietNam.

The XQ Da Lat Arts and Crafts Center is a cooperative honoring women and their work. In 1994, the cooperative received a commendation for restoring a traditional national art form through its training schools and professional classes. The cooperative also began a new phase in embroidery with works based on the theme of 'People's Lives in the Countryside of VietNam', a move from the traditional Royal Court themes in embroidery.

TOP LEFT A young Vietnamese woman works at her embroidery dressed in a traditional *ao dai*.

BOTTOM LEFT An exquisitely embroidered short silk jacket from the couture collections of Mai Lam Clothing in Ho Chi Minh City.

OPPOSITE Shading of colors in this silk embroidery on silk, fine-art piece from XQ DaLat Arts and Crafts Center, is a masterful accomplishment. The artist develops the gradations in colorations by selecting individual silk threads from an infinite variation of colors.

RIGHT These 21 designs form the image of a dragon rising—a powerful symbol of VietNam—enhanced by the rich imperial colors of these silk *ao dai* designed by HaNoi designer Le Lan Huong.

OPPOSITE *(bottom left) Ao dai* is de rigueur for many social occasions and the everyday dress of choice by many Vietnamese women. This shop offers *ao dai* made-to-measure from their many bolts of in-stock silks.

(bottom right) One of designer Le Lan Huong's collection for *ao dai* has pastoral scenes on satin silk. This cheerful *ao dai* design is displayed with a basket, pottery, and sheaves of rice—symbols of daily life in VietNam. The Le Lan Huong collection of wedding dresses is very beautiful.

Fashion: The Ao Dai of VietNam

The *ao dai* is the demure and sensual traditional dress of VietNam. It is made up of two parts: an ankle-length tunic with a front and back panel slit on each side from hem all the way up to the snug bodice which has tight-fitting sleeves. This form-fitting tunic opens on each side to expose the undergarment of loose-fitting trousers. It is a fetching sight to see young girls in their white *ao dai*, walking to school, the panels of their silk tunics fluttering in the breeze.

This style of traditional dress came about in the 1930s when a Vietnamese fashion designer known as Monsieur Le Mur lengthened the top of a traditional Vietnamese front-buttoned shirt so that it reached the floor, constructed a tight-fitting bodice and moved the buttons from the front to an opening along the shoulder and side seam. For important occasions, men wore a similar garment. Monsieur Le Mur adapted his design from the dress code imposed by Emperor Vu Vuong of the Nguyen dynasty in 1744, who decreed that men and women should wear a long, front-buttoned, knee-length shirt over trousers.

HaNoi fashion designer specializing in *ao dai* for weddings, Le Lan Huong says: "Becoming a fashion designer was my dream and now my dream has become true. When I design clothing, I am thinking it is like a work of art. It inherits genius to wear culture of our ancestors before and expresses a new beauty

of modern life. I would like to contribute my ability to maintain and develop the *ao dai* for the future. The best of all, I have a great wish: that all women in the world will know and like to wear the *ao dai*. I want to introduce the *ao dai* to international friends and dream about one day, the *ao dai* will flash on their streets". All of Lan Huong's *ao dai* designs are made in Vietnamese satin silk.

RIGHT Just sitting in the sun, protected by her *non*... the town well is a perfect place to sit and watch life go by in HoiAn.

BOTTOM RIGHT Varying slightly in shape from the Vietnamese *non*, this wide-brimmed *non ba tam* hat is the original type of hat worn in the old Tonkin (northern VietNam) region.

OPPOSITE Sea-worthy baskets—if traveling in harbors and rivers. These women in Nha Trang paddle to incoming fishing boats and bargain for the best of the catch, then hurriedly paddle back to the early morning fish market to sell their goods.

The art of basketry is taught to children at an early age and they often become part of the family business. Family members help manufacture items such as the very popular lanterns or various accessories for use in home interiors.

Basketry

Of all of the fabulous arts and crafts of Indochina, few can rival the artistry of basketry. The everyday needs of the people have been answered by basket weavers; there is an endless variety of baskets for work or play—for farming tools, fishing equipment including boats, toys, clothing, household goods— to name but a few. Rattan, bamboo, rush, reeds, and other natural materials have been used in practical, economical, and creative ways to produce baskets that are nothing short of works of art.

Probably no other single object is as quin-tessentially Indochinese as the *non*, the conical hat worn for protection against the sun or inevitable downpours. They are made from palm leaves that are softened by soaking in water, beaten then woven. The best part of a day is required to weave one hat.

LEFT Bamboo baskets for steaming delicate delicacies such as *bao* (dumplings).

ABOVE This traveling basket seller does not need a storefront to sell his wares.

Pottery

Pottery production is a millenniums-old craft in Indochina; techniques were learned from both India and China. Artefacts from the Cham and Khmer civilizations run the gamut of pottery, crockery and earthenware for the manufacture of utensils, tools, and sculpture. Potters in Northern VietNam worked from earliest times up until today, both in un-glazed pottery and in porcelain with glazes similar to those from China.

In this northern area, archeological sites have yielded stoneware dating from the 11th century, indicating an early tradition of firing beautiful hues of celadon. Schooners that sailed to European markets during the great maritime trade may well have carried cargos of ceramics from Indochina but were thought to be from China.

Today, there are several centers of production, most of which produce unglazed pottery fired at low temperatures. The northern region of VietNam in the Red River Delta has clay deposits of good quality and are known for finer ceramics with lovely glazes. Today, there are several centers of production, most of which produce unglazed pottery fired at low temperatures.

OPPOSITE **Off to the market with blue-and-white glazed pottery.**

BELOW **The village of Bat Trang near HaNoi has produced pottery for centuries, specializing in blue-and-white glazes fired at high temperatures. Motifs of flowers, dragons, and phoenixes are inherited from China, but the Vietnamese adaptations are lighter and more spontaneous.**

ABOVE Clay pots dry in the sun in the front yard of this potter's home near HoiAn. Wooden doors painted a vivid azure are common in the countryside of VietNam.

RIGHT Caught in the 'dance' of the art of pottery—two sisters work at the family business by taking turns at the pottery wheel shaping the pieces or spinning the wheel.

OPPOSITE In a village near HoiAn, the brick and earthen kiln is used cooperatively. The entire village works in ceramics, with the government lending a hand in marketing.

Lacquer

Glistening smooth lacquer work is as enchanting now as it was when the first treasured pieces arrived in Europe by way of sailing ships. Lacquer was an entirely new finish to Westerners but an age-old craft in Indochina. Objects made with lacquer coatings have been found in the Haiphong region, near the border of China, from as early as the 4th century.

Lacquer was initially used to preserve objects or to make porous surfaces waterproof; till today, some hill tribes continue to lacquer their teeth. Lacquer finishes became the rage in the West during the 17th and 18th centuries. Attempts were made by craftsmen in Europe and America to duplicate the quality of lacquer ware from the East, however they lacked a main ingredient—resins from the toxicodendron verniciflua tree of the cashew family—common to Indochina.

These resins, mixed with other chemicals, provide the base material to accomplish a hard finish on a wood or bamboo base. Lacquer ware became even more popular in the early 1900s with the advent of Art Nouveau, and later, Art Deco styles in the 1920s. The Paris Expo in 1925, exhibited sleek, angular, streamlined objects that satisfied the tastes of a post-World War I society. The highly polished lacquer finishes in bright and vibrant colours expressed the 'modern' feel of Art Deco. The fluid, spare lines of lacquer products were highly desirable in Europe at a time when products from the French colony of Indochina became increasingly available.

Lacquer production requires extraordinary skills in the application of multiple coats of thin resin under controlled conditions with polishing and sanding between applications. A well-made lacquered pro-duct is somewhat impervious to liquids.

RIGHT Handmade papers for sale by the sheet or made to order into attractive lanterns.

OPPOSITE Skillfully handmade paper with leaves and wild flowers added.

Paper Craft

Paper-making as an art and a craft is a specialty of Indochina. Paper craft is the art of making paper used for a variety of products such as umbrellas, household implements, lanterns, offerings, woodcut art, toys, and of course writing papers. Other cultures throughout the world have used bark to make a cloth used as paper, but 'true' paper-making techniques using wood and rice is a craft of Indochina that has a history of more than 2,500 years.

In the old quarter of HaNoi where, since the 13th century, 36 different guilds have operated on individual streets named after the type of products sold, Hang Giay sold only paper products, particularly specialty handmade papers.

The art of paper-making also includes innovative ideas to add variety in the colors, shapes, and textures to enhance the unique quality of hand-made sheets of finished paper. In Luang Prabang, paper craftsmen scatter natural objects such as leaves, petals, twigs, string, etc. throughout an individual sheet to add character. These beautiful papers are then used to make countless products.

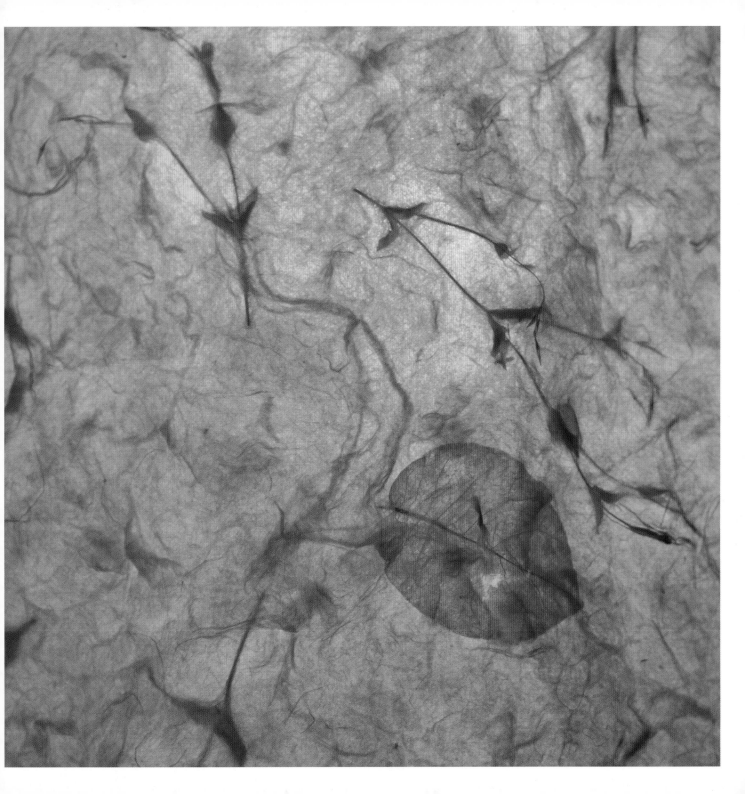

The Timbered Hall House

Timbered hall houses (as shown in photographs on pages 28, 60, 94, and 124) were places for study, contemplation and meetings. Commonly referred to as temples, a hall house always contained a sacred altar for performance of rituals in remembrance of honoured ancestors. Hall houses were part of a mandarin or a prosperous family property, but separate of the living quarters. Some villages have temples for meeting houses and the Temple of Literature in HaNoi, VietNam's first university, is a magnificent example of a temple built for higher learning.

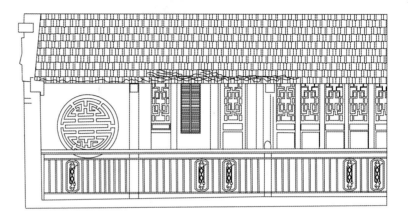

An interior view of an ancestral timbered hall house shows the strength and beauty of the exposed structure. Large post and beam timbers are joined using mortise and tenon techniques. Most of these handsome antique structures are easily dated by the year carved on a wooden centrepiece under the roof.

Columns are a large-diameter timber, usually planed to form a slightly tapered shape. Similar columns in Chinese architecture differ in that they were often constructed of many pieces of wood to form a single large column. Interior and exterior structural details are left exposed, including the underside of the roofing tiles and rafters. The finest of materials affordable were used in these revered structures assuring a lasting architectural heritage.

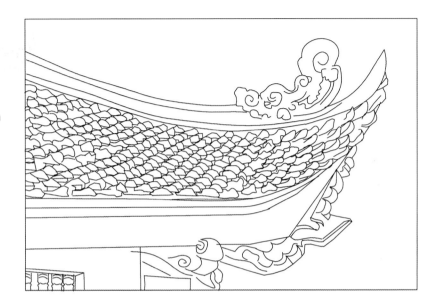

Roof designs of the timbered hall houses arch upward with a graceful lift. Mystical creatures are occasionally used to decorate the roofs, but more often designs are a gentle swirl of cloud-like forms.

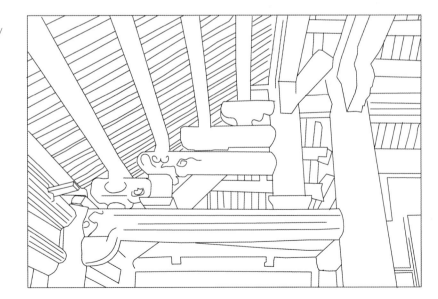

Timbers form structural roof supports to carry the weight of large overhangs. Please note the horizontal transfer beams are carved to a half-log shape from a square timber. The heft of the square beam adds interest to the whole composition, but is then slightly reduced in appearance by rounding the face of the beam and then further easing the mass with the upturned serif at the end. Vietnamese architecture is notable in the massive strength of materials contrasted by a quality of graceful lightness. Expert craftsmanship was required to accomplish the complicated joinery of this post and beam detail.

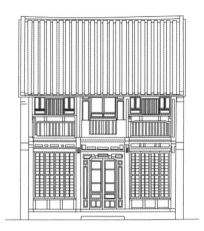

Tube Houses—An Urban Vernacular

Tube houses are a traditional style of urban dwellings named after the railroad-like shape (one-room about 3-5 meters wide with several consecutive rooms totaling 20-60 meters deep). To gain access from front to back of the tube house, it is necessary to pass through each of the rooms. Open-roofed courtyards separate rooms, allowing the penetration of air and light. The family business occupies the first floor space that opens directly onto the street; family living quarters are to the back or on the second or upper floors above the business. The second story room opening onto the street usually has a balcony to oversee the activity streetside. The Old Quarter in HaNoi has many examples of the classic old tube houses. See photographs on page 56 to 59 of the Thuy An Tailor Shop in HaNoi.

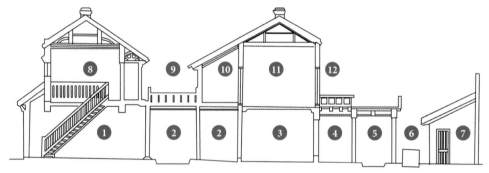

1. Business or shop area opening directly onto street

2. Rooms for business/storage/offices

3. 4. Family quarters/sleeping room for men and boys

5. Kitchen

6. Kitchen open courtyard, well for household water

7. Bathroom/toilet

8. Family Temple—altar for ancestors. Also the sitting room for men

9. Open courtyard

10. Work room for women's activities

11. Sleeping room for women and girls

12. Verandah

Tube houses in HoiAn dating from late 18th–19th Century are much the same as those in HaNoi. An interesting difference is that wood panels provide privacy and security when the shop is closed. Wide, horizontal boards slide into grooves in the casements of the shop windows. On page 58 is a street-scape view of HoiAn shop houses.

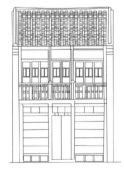

Cottage Style—Colonial Indochine

Cottage style dwellings constructed during the French Colonial period brought a new style of architecture to Indochina. Bricks or blocks were used rather than the customary wood or bamboo and a fusion of French, Lao, Cambodian, Chinese and Vietnamese elements appeared.

A cottage probably built for a French expatriate or a wealthy native mingles the Colonial taste with local influence.

Bannister and railing details are often constructed of mortar in a Colonial style, however wooden railing details are simplified and often have a geometric feeling with an Asian sensibility.

Mekong River Vernacular

Traveling along the Mekong from VietNam to Cambodian to Laos there are many styles of vernacular architecture, both wood and brick structures. In answer to seasonal floods during the monsoons, most structures are elevated. Typical Lao and Cambodian wooden houses along the river are built on stilts that rest on brick foundations—a proven structural solution for marshy lands. The upper floor houses the family while the ground floor space between the stilts is used for working, socializing and sheltering animals. The open design also keeps the house cool, allowing breezes to flow through, helping to clear the sultriness of high humidity.

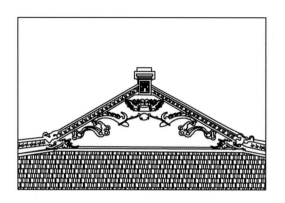

Colonial Details

Decorative motifs added at the roof peaks are often fanciful, designs in plasterwork mouldings while wood carvings may appear as eave details at the roof edges.

Colonial Indochine

A stucco and block villa style of the Colonial period is strongly influenced by European Classic architectural proportions, yet the bannister detail incorporates the Chinese ceramic vented tiles. These beautiful jade green tiles are ubiquitous in China and IndoChina, the Malay peninsular and throughout the Indonesian archipelago.

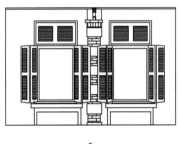
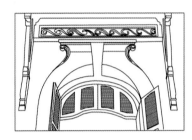
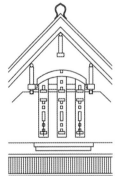

Vented transoms and wooden shutters are the favored window and door treatments in all of Indochina. Door openings frequently have both wood-louvered doors as well an additional set of solid wood doors that might have glass inserts.

France's early policy of 'assimilation' determined the French language, education system, laws and cultural style should prevail in the colony; however by the turn of the century, the theory was rejected as economically unsound and morally failed. A new theory of 'association' respected indigenous people and recognized their cultural differences. The emergence of Indochine style is linked to an international change in design and lifestyle preferences, a transition in the West from European Classicism to enthusiasm for things of an Oriental nature.

Chinoiserie Style flourished in Europe in the 18th and 19th centuries when respected craftsmen interpreted Chinese elements into their trade productions. Details such as faux-bamboo turnings and Chinese-like pierced fretwork were incorporated in furnishings, architecture, and the fine arts. The patterns in this document fabric of the period reveals the stylized concepts of what life in China might be.

Indochine Style designs were organic, appealingly natural and real in their simplicity. The furnishings made from native bamboo were genuine; they required no fret-worked details or faux-wood turnings to become other than they intrinsically 'are'. Indochine style represented the authentic. Motifs derived from the naturally occurring flora and fauna of Indochina appeared in textiles, arts and crafts.

This Chinoiserie fabric is typical of the fanciful style developed in the imaginations of European artisans. Their designs imagined delicate Chinese ladies and elderly mandarins in embroidered robes traipsing through an exotic landscape shared by birds and monkeys. Fabric shown is titled CochinChine, from the Braquenie' document collection of Pierre Frey Fabrics, Paris. The design is inspired by Jean Pillement, the 18th century "painter to the queen" and one of the first leading artists to take up the Rococo movement in Europe.

The design of this fabric illustrates the strong contrast between Chinoiserie Style and Indochine Style. In this pattern nature is depicted in a representative manner... in an open and flowing style. The design is elegant yet has a simplicity or purity in the content. There is a spirited panache more easily felt than described. The pattern is called Nakai, designed by Bernard Nevill, from the fabric collection of Pierre Frey, Paris.

Indochine Architecture: A blend of styles is seen in this early 20th century villa. European classic columns with vertical emphasis has been overruled by the definition and emphasis on horizontal lines, large overhangs and exposed rafter tail brackets in the eaves. The villa represents a less formal attitude in lifestyle.

Art Deco in Indochina

In Paris, the Exposition Internationale des Arts Décoratifs et Industriels Modernes, held in 1925 exposed the world to cutting edge French design of luxury goods that showcased motifs of the period termed Art Deco. Art Deco as a movement had begun in the early 1920's following the *fin de siecle* Art Nouveau period.

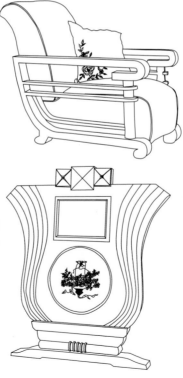

Indochine interpretations softened the edges of Chinoiserie and Art Nouveau, adding a lightness to the designs while managing to maintain the casual, unpretentious lifestyle of Indochina. The designs were instinctively fundamental, natural with sophisticated ease. At the height of the French colonization (early to mid-20th century), the Southeast Asians were enthusiastically utilizing Art Deco in their architecture, crafts, and furniture. These designs quickly merged into a style by the 1930's called Moderne.

Period Art deco furniture found through out Indochina used the flowing, curved shapes defining the style. Manufacturers of furniture in 21st century VietNam specialize in reproductions of the very popular Art Deco designs.

A 1920's French villa in HaNoi utilizes the nautical windows, parallel horizontal lines, curved shapes, and eyebrow canopy over windows of the Art Deco movement.